DAUGHTERS OF SPAIN

The Scottish novelist Joan Fallon, currently lives and works in the south of Spain. She writes both contemporary and historical fiction, and almost all her books have a strong female protagonist. She is the author of:

FICTION:
Spanish Lavender
The House on the Beach
Loving Harry
Santiago Tales
The Only Blue Door
Palette of Secrets
The Thread That Binds Us

The al-Andalus series:
The Shining City (Book 1)
The Eye of the Falcon (Book 2)
The Ring of Flames (Book 3)

(all are available in paperback and as ebooks)

Connect with her online at:

http:// www.joanfallon.co.uk

http://twitter.com/joan_fallon

https://www.facebook.com/joanfallonbooks

JOAN FALLON

DAUGHTERS OF SPAIN

An oral history:
snapshots of Spanish life through the recollections, hopes
and thoughts of the women of Spain.

Scott Publishing

© Copyright 2009
Joan Fallon

The right of Joan Fallon to be identified as the author of this
work has been asserted by her in accordance
with the Copyright, Designs and Patents Act 1988

All Rights Reserved

No reproduction, copy or transmission of this publication
may be made without written permission
No paragraph of this publication may be reproduced,
copied or transmitted save with the written permission
of the publisher, or in accordance with the
provisions of the Copyright Act 1956 (as amended)

Any person who commits any unauthorised act in
relation to this publication may be liable
to criminal prosecution and civil claims for damages.

ISBN 978-0-9576891-8-3
Published in 2014 by Scott Publishing
Windsor, England

First published in 2009 by Vanguard Press

DAUGHTERS OF SPAIN

This book is dedicated to all the women who gave so unsparingly of their time to talk to me about their past, their present and their future

Acknowledgements

This book would not have been possible without the willing participation of the women interviewed. I would like to thank them all for giving so generously of their time, for their patience and their openness.

My thanks also go to my kind friends who took the trouble to read numerous drafts of the book.

'This is still difficult for me to talk about; it caused me so much suffering. Well when the baby was born and I went to register her they wanted to put my husband's name on the birth certificate. I told them that they couldn't do that because he was not the father. They said if I wanted my name on the birth certificate I also had to have my husband's name. We argued for a bit then they asked me the name of the baby's father. I told them and they wrote his name in as the father and put the mother as unknown. I told them that it was wrong; that I was the mother, but they wouldn't listen. How could they put "mother unknown", when I was standing there right in front of them?' **Jeannette.**

'It was not a very big college; in our class there were about eight boys and fourteen girls. The girls were allowed to study alongside the boys but during the breaks we were kept separate. One day, when I was eighteen years old, a boy in my class offered me a lift home in his car. We were just leaving the car-park when an armed policeman stopped us and pointed his gun into the car and told me to get out. He said I was not allowed to leave the college in the company of a boy. I tried to protest but he just kept waving his gun at me so in the end I got out and went to wait for the bus.' **Pilar.**

'Am I happy? Yes, I'm happy with what I've done, but truly happy? I don't know. At least now I make the decisions; first it was my father making decisions for me, then my boyfriend, then my husband; now I make the decisions.' **Mari Jesus**.

Introduction

This book attempts to give the reader a flavour of what life was like for Spanish women during the last seventy years, from the beginning of the Civil War until the present day, from a totalitarian dictatorship to a socialist democracy. Through a series of conversations with women of all ages, we learn of their aspirations, fears and disappointments, their joys and their successes. Together they create a mosaic of the lives of mothers, daughters and grandmothers.

At the beginning of the twentieth century women in Spain lived closely regulated and restrictive lives, far similar to the lives of Muslim women than their northern European counterparts; according to Laurie Lee when he visited southern Spain as a young man in the 1930s, some women even veiled their faces. Women had no independence and were totally under the control of either their fathers or their husbands; they could be given away in arranged marriages and were never allowed out without chaperones. They were forbidden to have their own bank accounts or property, even when they were married. If they wanted a passport they had to have the permission of their father or husband.

Life for working-class women was even worse; those that worked on the land worked from sunrise to sunset then had to go home to cook, clean and care for their children. Even when they did the same work as men they were only paid half the wages that the men received, one and a half pesetas a day; it was "women's wages" whether it was "women's work" or men's.

The Second Republic

The Second Republic, which was in power from 1931 to 1936, introduced some limited reforms which benefitted women. In the 1931 Constitution women were awarded the vote and given full legal status within the state. Then the government passed a number of laws on divorce and civil marriage; adultery became no longer a crime and abortion was legalised. Women were allowed free access to the labour market and some limited maternity leave, and the length of the working day was reduced to eight hours, leaving women with more time to work in the home.

The first changes began with the collectives that were formed during the Second Republic, where women worked alongside men and for the first time found they had equal rights. In many collectives they were paid the same money as the men but even then most were paid a "family wage", which was given directly to the head of the family, the husband. The collectives had sprung up in the northern part of Spain as a result of many years of anarchist propaganda in the countryside. By mutual agreement many groups of peasants with their own smallholdings agreed to work together and share the profits of their labour. By 1936 these communes, or collectives as they were locally known, were more structured and each village had an elected management committee that was responsible for the economic administration of the commune. Work was obligatory for all men between the ages of eighteen and sixty; they were formed into groups of ten or so and given specific areas to farm or jobs to do. The workers reported back to the committee on the progress that was being made and they were given a "producer's" card on which they recorded the hours they had worked. These hours worked were converted into a number of units to be used as a means of exchange to obtain goods from the communal shops. Everything other than personal family items, such as clothing and furniture, was put into a communal pool to be shared according to a family's needs, while other necessities such as electricity, rent, medical care, education and pharmaceuticals were free. Non-workers such as the sick and the elderly received a "consumer's" card so that they too could receive a share of the produce. Even artisans such as hairdressers, cobblers and bakers formed themselves into collectives. Schools were set up in abandoned convents and all children had to attend until the age of fourteen; they were not allowed to work before then. It was in these collectives that women first realised that they could have a say in what was happening around them, although even there they were still not always assured of an equal vote with the men.

ADELE born in Málaga in 1959

Adele was born in Málaga in 1959 and has lived in and around the village of Benajarafe Alto all her life. She is 49 years old, married and has two grown-up children. She works as a cleaner for some the foreign residents who live nearby.

Adele arrived one afternoon on her moped; she had finished work for the day and had managed to find me a couple of hours before she began to prepare the evening meal for her husband and two children. She lived in a small hamlet called Los Nezas and worked as a cleaner in the houses of nearby residents, most of whom were foreigners, Danish or English.

'My mother was born in 1919 in Los Puertas, a small village about five kilometres from here,' she began.

I knew the village she meant; it was a group of white painted houses that nestled on the side of a hill, sheltered from both the cold, north wind in winter and the heat of the afternoon sun in summer.

'She had three sisters and a brother; quite a small family in those days. My grandfather owned a bakery and every week he would go with his donkey to the nearby town, Almayate, to buy flour and my grandmother made the dough at night ready to cook first thing in the morning. They also had a small market garden and grew lots of produce: beans, tomatoes, peas and peppers. They sold bread and goats' cheese, which my grandmother also made. A lot of the crops did not need watering, such as the beans and the peas, but it was my mother's job to water the tomatoes and peppers and when she was very small she and her brother and sisters took it in turn to help with the *noria*, a waterwheel that pumped the water up into our well. It was powered by the donkey, which walked round and round in a circle until the well was full.

One of the children had to sit there until there was enough water and then untie the donkey otherwise he would just keep on walking forever. From a very young age my mother had to help with everything, in the *huerta*, the vegetable garden, in the house and in the bakery.

She and her sister began to work on the *fincas,* or local farms, when they were twelve years old and they were paid by the day. They worked during the harvests, picking tomatoes, olives, almonds, whatever was in season. There were no *invernaderos*, greenhouses, then; everything was grown in its season. The pickers went out in teams of four or five with one of them acting as the leader. They worked in the fields all year round and in summer it was hard, hot work. They worked *de sol a sol*, from sunrise to sunset and then they still had to help at home, working in the bakery or the house. Even after she was married my mother continued working as a picker on the farms.

One of my mother's sisters, my aunt Loli, moved to Madrid when she married because she had a child with asthma and the doctor recommended that she move away from the sea. Another sister, my aunt Maria, moved to Badajoz, where her husband had an uncle with a hire-purchase business. It was a shop which sold everything from furniture to clothes and people bought what they needed and paid bit by bit. So he and my aunt worked there. The third sister remained fairly close to home, in Almayate and my mother's brother left home at an early age and went to Algeciras to be a fisherman. He was a rather rebellious young man and didn't keep in touch with the family until he was an old man, then he went to live with one of his sisters; he never married.

My mother and her brother and sisters went to the local school, where they had a very basic education but none of them stayed there very long; they were all needed to work. The school is still there, you know, and has about twenty pupils,' she added.

'And my grandmother's house is still there, but I don't know the people who live in it nowadays. My grandmother came to live with us when she became old. I remember her being very particular with her appearance; every morning she would wash herself thoroughly in a china bowl that stood in a big wooden stand that she had brought from her own house. Then she would comb her hair, which was so long that she could sit on it, for hours before pinning it up on top of her head. She told me that when my great-grandmother died she had to wear black for two years and stockings and a scarf all the time, even when working in the fields. It was strange about the headscarf: it had a peak and if the dead person was a close relative than the peak was much longer than usual. If your husband had died you wore the scarf with a very long peak but if it was a cousin you hardly needed to make any peak at all. The other thing she told me was that during the period of *luto*, mourning, the door to your house had to remain closed; you were not allowed to have visitors. To leave the door open was a lack of respect. My grandmother died when I was sixteen; she was eighty-five.

According to my grandmother things were pretty bad during the war; many people went hungry and food was rationed. Things were not so bad for their family because they had the bakery and their garden, but others were not so lucky. She could remember the monks giving out rations of powdered milk to the poor at the church. My grandfather was too old to fight in the war but my father fought for the

Nationalists and one of his brothers was killed. I know my father fought in many places, Melilla and Madrid and others I can't remember. Now whenever we see one of these places on the TV he tells me that he was there. He can remember it all despite the fact that he's ninety-one.

It was when he came back from the war that my father began to court my mother. He lived in a nearby village called Benajarafe Alto and his father kept goats. One of his brothers had married a girl from Los Puertas and one day he told my father he had seen this very nice girl that he thought my father would like, so my father went to the village to see for himself. In those days the country people did the *rueda*; it was a custom where everyone sat in a big circle, singing and clapping then one of the men would get up and walk over to one of the girls and ask her to dance in the *rueda*, the circle, with him. That was how my father met my mother; he asked her to dance. I suppose he had gone to the village with the intention of finding a bride because very soon after that he went to my grandparents' house to ask for her hand; this gave him the right to visit her in her home. They became *novios*, engaged, but they never went out together, except once a year and then my grandparents went with them. My father walked the four and a half kilometres across the hills to Los Puertas every Sunday, Wednesday and Friday to visit her; those were the only days he was allowed to see her.   He did this for eleven years before they were married. In those days lots of the men wore rope sandals and my mother told me that one day my father was climbing the Cuesta de Rosita and his sandal broke so he had to walk the rest of the way to her village barefoot.'

I thought of the stony land around there and winced.

'Anyway,' continued Adele. 'They got married in the little church in Benjarafe Alto and they and their guests walked the four kilometres from Los Puertas to the church. My father had bought two rooms in his mother's house for them to live in: a kitchen and a bedroom. He paid his mother a little every week until the rooms were paid for; he never wanted to rent anywhere. My father worked on the land and helped his father with the goats. I remember that we could go and milk the goats whenever we wanted any milk. Most of the milk was used to make cheese but we could drink what was over.

My mother continued working after she married and even after she had me she worked at harvest time. I wasn't born until she was forty. She had had a very bad time with her first baby who was born stillborn, so she had to go to the Hospital Civil in Málaga for the birth. So because of that I was an only child; she never had any more. She told me she had the same two dresses for the whole year: one for working and one for going out and in the winter she wore a cardigan over them to keep warm. They were all the clothes she had.

I don't know whether my father liked her working but I do know that when I left school and started work he was not happy. He asked me why I needed to work when I had everything at home.

I went to the local school for a couple of years and then my parents sent me to La Marina, a public school in Torre de Benagalbon. I used to pick up the school bus every day outside the cemetery and it would bring me home again in the evening. Curiously my husband went to the same school but he was a boarder so I never knew him then even though by then the boys and girls were all in the same class. When I was fourteen I left school and went to work in the Hotel Esperanza.

I used to walk to work and back each day, two and a half kilometres each way. I was very lucky to get work in the hotel because it was much nicer work than in the fields; it was cleaner and cooler. My friend who was already working there had put in a word for me and I began in the laundry room. Later on I worked in the mornings as a chamber maid and in the afternoons in the laundry. We had twenty-one rooms to clean between the two of us and it was hard work but you could have the windows open and it was cool and fresh. The afternoons were worse because it was so hot and steamy in the laundry, especially when we began using the steam iron. When I had my holidays I didn't go away I worked in the fields picking whatever was in season to earn extra money. I worked like that for nine years until my first child was born.

I met my husband at the *Misa de Franco*. It was just after Franco died and they held a Mass in the new church in Benajarafe. We all got dressed up and walked down to the church; people came from all the local villages and the church was packed. It wasn't that people were sad that Franco had died it was because there were so few opportunities to go out in those days that any occasion was welcomed. Well on the way down the hill I saw this boy trying to fix his moped which had broken down on the side of the road. My mother knew his family so we stopped and spoke for a while. Then a few days later my cousin came to see me and told me that this boy fancied me. The next thing was that he came to my house to see if we could go out together. It wasn't the same as in my mother's day we didn't have to stay in the house all the time but we still didn't go out a lot, maybe twice a month; sometimes we would go out on his moped but never very far.

Even then I was not allowed to stay out very late, about eleven o'clock in the winter and a little later in the summer. We were engaged for nine years.'

She stopped and took a drink of water then continued:

'Do you know I never had a bathroom until we got married. In my parents' house it was always my job to get the water and I had to bring in two buckets, one for the kitchen and one we left by the front door. I bathed in an old enamel bath with a hose. We had no running water and no taps in that house.

It's so different now. My daughter still lives at home; she's twenty-two and studying Business Studies. She never helps me with anything because she says she is too busy with her studies but I always had to help my mother with the housework, even when I was working myself.

I have two children, but the boy is younger. I want them both to study. When I was young I was not very keen on studying and now I wish I had. Nowadays it's more important because if you don't study you won't get a job. In my day there were more open fields; you could always work on the land. But now there's nothing. And besides there are few people who want to work on the land; they leave it to the immigrants. But if you want to work in a hotel or an office you need to study.

My daughter has so much more freedom than I did. Last Saturday she left home at five in the evening and then telephoned me to say she would be spending Sunday on the beach, so she wouldn't be home until Sunday evening. Mind you she never did that until she became eighteen. Now I think well it's up to her what she does.

She has been going out with the same boyfriend since she was seventeen and I think she would like to get married but he's not interested in marriage. He's not very religious. I don't mind if they get married or not; they can do what they want. We're not a very religious family but I do go to Mass at least once a month.

Franco 1939-1975

When the Popular Front was elected in 1936 and formed a government, the Spanish Right considered that to be the first step towards a revolution. In fact in the end the revolution began as a counter-attack against Franco and his generals. The Civil War of 1936-1939 that ensued and Franco's ultimate victory put an end to all the changes implemented by the Second Republic and women's rights were set back forty years. The collectives were destroyed and the new laws repealed; women's short taste of independence was hastily removed and the old order for women was reinstated. Spanish women were to emulate the Virgin Mary and be good wives and mothers, or nuns.

Some Francoist school textbooks that have been recently re-printed provide some interesting insights on the official attitude towards women at the time. They state that "women lack creative talents, which God has reserved for men" and that women "have never discovered anything", obviously forgetting about Marie Curie and many others. They go on to inform the students that "a wife has no rights over her own body. On marriage she gives up the rights to her husband. He is the only one who can use those rights and only for reproduction."

ARACELI born in Malaga in 1918

Araceli has just celebrated her ninetieth birthday. She is a widow and has one daughter and one granddaughter. She was born in Málaga and lived there during the Civil War before moving to Portugal to get married. She and her husband lived in Portugal for a number of years before moving back to Spain. She has never worked. Now she lives in a flat next door to her daughter.

Araceli preferred to talk to me in her daughter's apartment, even though she lived on the floor above. She came down just as Paola was serving the coffee. She was a small woman, but sprightly for her age and her back was upright and strong; she had dressed as if she was going into town, with a smart, blue dress, covered in red flowers. Her hair was carefully combed and she had applied some make-up. She was obviously looking forward to talking to me about her life and began straight away:

'I was eighteen when the Civil War broke out and I was living in Málaga with my parents. As soon as the bombing started my uncle invited us to go and stay with him in the *Camino de Antequerra*, which was just outside the city.'

She smiled, causing the wrinkles around her bright blue eyes to multiply and explained:

'That's actually near the main hospital now, but in those days the city was much smaller. If we went up on to the roof of my uncle's house we could still see the planes dropping their bombs on Málaga, and the smoke from the fires, but we felt a bit safer there. The house had a *refugio* in the garden, a sort of air-raid shelter built under the ground. Whenever they rang the church bells in warning we would run to the shelter, but I hated going inside because of the smell. It was dark and very crowded with all our neighbours and there was nowhere to sit; we had to sit on the ground. We would be in there for hours and there was no water and nothing to eat. We had some chickens for a while and one day we made a big *tortilla* with the eggs and took it down with us.'

She wrinkled her nose at the memory and added:

'It was a bit dry, but we were glad of it. There wasn't much food in the shops at that time. Every day it was my brother's job to go and queue for bread; sometimes he had to wait a long time to get any.

I remember watching the soldiers go by. *Los Rojos,* as we called them, "the Reds", didn't wear uniforms, but they had red flags and some of them wore red scarves around their necks. The *Nacionalistas.*'

She stopped to check I understood the difference between the two sides, then continued:

'The *Nacionalistas* were very smart in their uniforms; I remember seeing them come over the mountains with the Italian troops. Some were on horseback or walking, but a lot were in big lorries that blocked the streets. We were pleased to see them; we didn't like *Los Rojos.* We hoped they would sort them out. I never once saw the African troops, but I heard about them. They said that they entered the city from a different route and they were very fierce, killing anyone who got in their way.

Lots of families had one son who was on the side of the *Nacionalistas* and one on the side of the *Rojos*, but we were all *Nacionalistas* in my family. I was a *Falangista,* a youth member of the *Falange*; at first my job was to sew soldiers' uniforms. They would bring me the material and all the buttons, badges and epaulets in a packet. I learnt to cut out the uniforms and sew them, but I wasn't very good at it. Then later I worked in a canteen, serving food to the orphans. In those days it was voluntary service, designed to help the war effort, but later, under Franco, it became compulsory social service for women. It was similar to the military conscription for men, but women only had to work for six months, helping in the orphanages or health clinics or in schools. If you didn't do it you couldn't get a passport or a driver's licence. It lasted until the 1970s.'

She looked across at her daughter and added:

'Paola didn't have to do it; she was born in Portugal.'

Then she continued:

'Well, my sister wanted to join the *Falangistas* as well, but she was too young; you had to be eighteen, so she joined *Las Flechas,* (The Arrows), a *Falange* youth group for the under eighteens. She only joined so she could go to dance classes,' she added dismissively.

'My father did not join the army; he was too old to fight, he had not got married until he was thirty-six, but my uncle went to the front.

At the beginning of the war lots of people from the villages came to Málaga, which was in the Republican zone, hoping to get away from the Nationalist troops, and the city was crowded with homeless people. Nobody went out at night because you were frightened you would be killed. You heard such awful stories: one night a man found a baby abandoned in the street. He had nine children of his own, and he couldn't feed another one, so he advertised for a home for it. Someone came and took the baby away. Lots of children were lost then; it was so easy to lose a child in all that chaos. Another story we heard was that *Los Rojos* had kidnapped the son of a Nationalist general and promised to release him if the general surrendered. He refused, so they shot his son. Then there was an Englishman who helped some nuns to escape by taking them in his yacht to Gibraltar. He was frightened that *Los Rojos* would kill them, because there were rumours of nuns being soaked in petrol and burnt alive. There were so many stories you didn't know which to believe.

Calle Larios, the main street, suffered lots of damage; houses were burnt and bombed, shops were looted and their goods piled up in the streets and burned. It was very dangerous to go out, but I only ever saw one dead person; he was lying in the street and everyone was running away. I remember he wore a white shirt and had blond hair; his face was very handsome.'

She stopped, thinking about it, then said:

'There was a joke they told then; can I tell you it?'

I nodded and she began:

'There were three young men walking down Calle Larios, when a soldier approached them. He stopped the first one and asked:

'Which party do you belong to?'

The man replied replied: 'Communist.'

So the soldier beat him up.

He turned to the second young man and asked:

'Which party do you belong to?'

He replied: 'Nationalist.'

And the soldier beat him up too.

Then the third young man was asked:

'Which party do you belong to?'

And he replied:

'Just get on with it and beat me."

She giggled, making sure I understood the joke, then continued:

'That's what it was like then. Some of the richer people sent their children away to France or Germany just to be safe.'

Her daughter came in carrying a tray with glasses of water and a dish of muscatel grapes.

'Some refreshment?' she asked.

Her mother drank the water gratefully then suggested she tell me something of her life after the war.

'I never had many boyfriends; there was one during the war, who joined up and went to fight with the *Nacionalistas*, but although he wrote to me from time to time, it never came to anything.

I remember that in those days they closed *Calle Larios* to traffic at six o'clock and all the young people would walk up and down with their friends, for hours and hours, just chatting and looking at everyone; it was the thing to do, then. Sometimes we would go into a café and order cakes and sweet Málaga wine. Some days we spent the afternoons dancing; my friend knew three brothers, one played the guitar, the other the violin and the third the accordion and they would come to her house and play for us.'

At this point her daughter interrupted:

'Do you remember when I went to Tetuan last year?'

Her mother nodded.

'Well it was just like that. It reminded me of Málaga forty years ago, everybody walking up and down the main street, all the single people looking for people of the opposite sex. The only difference was that they don't drink alcohol in Morocco, so instead of bars there were loads of tea and cake shops.'

'Well as I remember it there were lots of soldiers in Málaga in those days and foreigners as well, but I never went out with any of them.

Strolling down Calle Larios

My sister went to Portugal to get married. Her husband was half Spanish and half Portuguese; he lived in Portugal but his parents had separated and his father had returned to Málaga to live. That's how she met her husband; he was in Málaga visiting his father at the time. Anyway when she moved to Portugal she kept writing to me asking me to go to visit her but my father didn't want me to go and to be truthful I didn't really want to go either. But she kept on writing; she said she wanted me to meet a friend of her husband's, who was very nice and was unmarried. So in the end I became curious about this man and I said I would go. I had to get a passport and I also had to have my father's permission to travel. In the end he agreed that I could go and I went by train to Portugal. The passport was only valid for two months and I had to give it up when I returned to Málaga.

Well I liked this man straight away and of course we became *novios*. Naturally once we were engaged I was not allowed to go out with anyone else, not even my girlfriends; no more walks down *Calle Larios*. We were married in Portugal and we lived there for the first years of our marriage. My husband was an economist and earned a good living. He was a fantastic man; each year he would remember the day we met and he would bring me little presents on the anniversary. The first time he brought me a box of sweetmeats, I asked him what they were for. I said: "What day is it then?" and he replied: "Don't you know?" I said: "Well it's not my *Santo* and it's not my birthday." Then I realised it was the day we had met. He always remembered, every year.

He used to like to know where I was and when I'd be home; if I went out and realised I was going to be late I would ring his company and ask his secretary to tell him that his wife would be late home. He never minded if I was late as long as he knew, but if I didn't ring and he arrived home and there was no food on the table he was not happy. He really looked after me; he never wanted me to work. Even at home I had a girl to help in the house.'

Araceli paused and wiped her eyes; talking about her dead husband made her sad. Then she continued:

'Before I met him, I worked for a short while in the office of an Italian. He was a very tall, handsome man and my father heard rumours that he was having an affair with one of his secretaries, so he took me away and wouldn't let me work there anymore.'

'Were you very religious?' I asked her.

'No, not really, but I went to Mass, the majority of people did in those days. My husband wasn't religious; he would escort me to the door of the church but he wouldn't go in.

Araceli and her brother at their first communion

We were brought up in religious schools; my sister and I were taught by the nuns and my brother went to the *Maristas*. My mother was always very friendly with the nuns. When I was younger I liked to go to church because it was a social occasion and I always went with my friends. The priest was very strict. We weren't allowed to wear any make-up to church or show any bare skin; all the girls had to wear veils. We each had a different coloured veil and we would exchange them, so that each week we could wear a different colour. When it was *Semana Santa* we would dress up in our best frocks and wear a mantilla in our hair and we would walk to the church barefoot, carrying our best shoes in our hands so they didn't get dusty. I remember one year our priest's sister, well she was actually a friend of his from Cordoba, came to visit him during *Semana Santa*. She was really surprised to see us wearing the mantilla; she had never seen one before.

Friends posing for a photograph in the park.

Semana Santa

The priest used to have a lot of power; he and the mayor were the most important people in the village but they often disagreed about things. One year there was a dispute about where they would display *el Cruz de Mayo*, the May Cross; the whole village split into two groups. One group wanted it displayed in the church as usual and the other in the school. The cross was large and made of flowers and every 3rd of May it was paraded through the village and then put in the church. That particular year the mayor insisted that the May Cross was to be put up in the school. The priest was so annoyed that he stormed into the school, picked up the cross and threw it onto the floor, smashing it. Everybody was amazed but nobody did anything about it.'

'What about Paola?' I asked.

'Paola was born while we still lived in Portugal, before we moved to Casas de Don Pedro in Extramadura,' she said. 'But Paola can tell you about that.'

The Falange and the Sección Femenina

The Spanish Falange was founded by José Antonio Primo de Rivera, son of the right-wing dictator, Miguel Primo de Rivera in 1933. Its aim was to promote a strong, united nationalism within the state and to impose a rigorous discipline on education. It condemned socialism, communism, republicanism and capitalism and promoted fascism, modelled on the Italian fascist state.

When the Spanish Civil War broke out in 1936 the Falange sided with Franco but José Antonio was captured and put to death in November of that year leaving the party without a leader. In 1937 Franco merged the Falange with the Carlists and renamed them the Falange Española Tradicionalista and made it the official party of the Nationalist State.

The plan of the Falange was always to return Spain to the days before the Second Republic and central to this plan was the role of women. There was a strict divide between the men who were to produce a new nation and the women who were to bear the nation's sons.

A youth section called Las Flechas was set up and members were urged to participate in physical education and sport; the first rally took place in Seville in October 1938 where 1,600 girls and adolescents gave a display of gymnastics and dancing. Not everyone was happy at the thought of young women participating in sport and the Church spoke out against it. However women were limited to taking part in what were deemed "appropriate sports", such as swimming, tennis and gymnastics; these were referred to as "beauty sports". Any sport with a more masculine side was discouraged and the emphasis was always on refinement, self-control and modesty.

José Antonio's sister, Pilar Primo de Rivera started the Sección Femenina with the aim of teaching women how to be "good patriots, good Christians and good wives". Most middle-class wives were expected to participate in some sort of social service in the Sección Femenina: helping in canteens, or schools or health clinics and encouraged to intervene in the lives of other women and ensure their compliance with the State. At the time the social service was considered to be a war-time necessity but it continued after the war was over and became compulsory. If a woman did not complete her six months social service she was unable to get a passport, a driving licence or receive a university degree. Before undertaking her stint of social service the woman was also expected to do a period of intensive training with the leaders of the Sección Femenina, priests and doctors. The women were taught about childcare, housekeeping and other feminine tasks and indoctrinated with anti-liberalist literature. Although Pilar Primo de Rivera wanted women to have training in social work and nursing, her group strongly promoted the idea that women should marry and produce children for "the fatherland". That was to be their main role in life.

DOLORES born in Rio Gordo in 1926

Dolores (Lola) was born in the village of Rio Gordo and moved to Málaga when she married. She is 83 years old and has two married children. She still lives in Málaga with her husband. She never worked other than as a housewife.

Lola is the mother of one of my best friends. He said she would be delighted to see me and talk about the old days.

'Come in the evening,' he said. 'Pick me up around seven and I'll take you round there. They are staying in their summer house at the moment.'

We drove through a tangle of streets on a small urbanisation overlooking the Mediterranean. His mother was sitting at a round table in the garden, with her husband and her daughter. She was a comfortably built woman, not very tall and her grey hair had been rinsed blonde; she looked about sixty-five, but admitted to being eighty-three.

'*Bienvenida*,' she said, kissing me on both cheeks.

They all got up in turn and kissed me, made me sit down in the shade and offered me tea. While Lola's daughter went into the house to make it we talked politely about the weather, then I set up my voice recorder and began to ask Lola about her life.

'Were you born in Malaga, Lola?' I began.

'No, I was born in Rio Gordo. Do you know Rio Gordo?'

I nodded.

'*Semana Santa* is wonderful there. You have to visit it in *Semana Santa*, it is very special, everyone in their beautiful dresses and all the processions,' she said, smiling proudly.

Rio Gordo is a village of white-washed houses and red roofs, located in the north of the province of Málaga. It nestles below the Sierra Camorolas, and the crystal clear water that flows down from the mountains gathers in the Rio de la Cueva, the river that runs through the centre of the village, feeding the flour mills. It is harsh countryside; the air hangs hot and dry over the village in the summer and in the winter, despite the sun that continues to shine, a cold wind blows down from the snow capped mountains. The village is surrounded by olive groves and plantations of almond trees, while further out fields of cereals cover the lower slopes of the mountains. The deep valleys are lined with eucalyptus and scarlet-tipped oleanders. It has the feel of a village that has always been prosperous, with its tall buildings and ornate balconies.

Lola began to tell me what it was like to grow up there:

'Well you know Andalucia was very poor in those days; there was no industry in our area, only a few factories to process the olives and eight or nine flour mills. Our village was very quiet; there were three flour mills, a small olive oil processing plant, a school and a church. My father was a builder and when he was old enough my brother became a builder too. I was the eldest of four children, two boys and two girls. There was always plenty of food in our house; even during the war we never went short of food or clothes. Well I don't remember us going short of anything, but I was only ten when it began. In fact I don't remember our village being really affected by the war at all. We saw some people heading for Almeria one day, trying to get away from the fighting, but we never really saw any troops.

My husband was from Rio Gordo too; his father was a miller, he had one of the flour mills in the village, so there was always plenty of bread. Originally the mill was called the Molino de las Tablas, but then it was renamed Molino de la Virgen de Belén because one day his father was working on the land and he found a picture of the Virgin Mary in the ground near the mill. He made a stone niche for it and set it up as a shrine and people came to light candles and say a quick prayer to the Virgen. Later when the electricity came to the village he ran a cable to light it.

I went to the local school. It was for all the village children, but the boys and girls were kept strictly separated. The girls didn't really get much opportunity to study; they had very poor education really and were only allowed to stay in school until they were eight or nine. When the time came for my friends and me to leave our teacher told us that we could continue to attend every day, but if the school inspector came we had to stay at home for the day.'

'It wasn't until the Act of 1970 that education became compulsory for children from the age of six to fourteen,' her husband interjected. 'But even then there were hundreds of children that never learnt to read and write.'

'Of course the boys were allowed to stay in school longer. My husband was lucky,' Lola continued, smiling at her husband. 'His father was quite well off and didn't want his son to work in the fields like most of the other boys, so he sent him to Málaga to continue his studies. I remember him telling me that he stayed with a family, in a small boarding house and they gave him boquerones every day for both lunch and dinner. Those small fish are very good for you, but every day? I ask you.

I met my husband, Laureano when I was only sixteen; he was my first boyfriend. I used to see him in the village but we never spoke; then one day when I was walking through the village with my friend and he was walking behind with his cousin he began to talk to me and suggested we become *novios*. A few days later he waited until he saw my father come out of our house and he went up to speak to him to ask if he could ask me to marry him. My father was quite agreeable about it but Laureano had to make a formal proposal to me. He arranged to visit me at home very soon. At least he came and asked me to my face; his own father had proposed to his mother by letter. Anyway I told him I'd think about it. No-one ever said yes straight away; it wasn't the custom. He had to return the next evening to see what my reply was. Of course then I said yes. We were engaged for eleven years.

Lola before she was married

When Laureano visited the house we sat in the parlour at the "*mesa camilla*", a round table covered in a heavy cloth, him on one side and me on the other; my mother sat to one side watching every move we made. We were not allowed to touch, not even hold hands; they made sure we were never left on our own, ever. When the weather was cold my mother would put some hot coals in a round, copper brazier and put it underneath the table. We sat with our feet and legs under the tablecloth; it was lovely and warm like that.

Laureano went away to study first and then to work, and I remained at home with my mother preparing myself for married life. He would come home sometimes at weekends, always at Christmas and Easter and for his holidays in the summer. Sometimes I would go to Málaga to stay with my aunt and buy the material and threads that I needed to make my wedding trousseau. I made it all by hand and I stitched and embroidered sheets, bolster covers, tablecloths, curtains, everything I would need in my own home. You couldn't buy many things then. I spent months and months sewing, and all my friends were the same. My mother also taught me to cook and look after the house; she wrote down lots of recipes for me.

My sister also became engaged but she never got married; she was engaged for forty years. Her fiancé lived at home with his mother and an aunt; he told her that he wanted to get married, but he never did anything about it. I think he was too tied to his mother and her sister and by the time they had both died my sister felt it was too late for them to get married, so they lived together for a while.

When Laureano came home he continued to visit me at my house, with my mother present or sometimes we would meet in the Plaza Real by the bridge and walk down to the main road and back again. All the young people did that. There was not much else to do in our village. We all loved dancing though and we had lots of dances in people's houses. There was a boy who played the guitar and another who played the *bandurria*, that's like a guitar, but smaller. Once a week we would go to a bar in the town that had a dance hall and dance the *pasodoble.* There were the *ferias*, and of course we celebrated Christmas and *Semana Santa* and all the saints' days. We didn't have much then but I don't remember feeling deprived. I suppose I'm the sort of person who is happy with what they've got.

I used to go to Mass every week; all the women went, but not many of the men bothered. In the church the women sat on the left and the men on the right. All the women had to cover their arms and heads before they went into the church or the priest would send you out. The priest was very important in the village; he, the mayor and the doctor, they were the most powerful people in the community. There were three or four influential families; families with lots of money and land. And there was also a midwife, but she was not trained, she was really just a woman with lots of experience at delivering babies.

When we got married we had to have a very simple wedding because my grandmother had died three months before and the celebrations had to be kept to a minimum. My mother was not allowed to attend my wedding because she was still in mourning. She couldn't even come to the church. In those days, particularly in the countryside, you dressed completely in black when you were in mourning and it lasted a specified length of time according to your relationship to the deceased. Sometimes women could not get out of mourning for years as one death succeeded another: cousins, uncles, aunts, second cousins, it could go on forever. We were married in the village church by the local priest and then we walked through the village streets, with all the local children running alongside singing this rhyme:

"Padrino, lagarto
Eche usted los curators
No los gaste en vino
Que es un borrachino."

("Lively lad
Throw us your money
Don't spend it on wine
Which will only make you drunk.")

It was traditional to throw money to the children, and we laughed because the streets were cobbled and the children had a lot of difficulty picking up the coins.

I said then that if we lived to see our golden wedding anniversary we would celebrate it in style. So a few years ago we had a second wedding; we went to the church and renewed our vows and all the family attended, even relatives from Madrid and the Canaries. That time we had a proper celebration.'

She stopped while her daughter showed me the photographs of the ceremony then continued:

'Well as I was saying, we got married and we went by train to Seville and then on to Madrid for our honeymoon. We had some relatives in Madrid, but in Seville we stayed in a hotel. I remember when we signed the hotel register, the concierge made some comment about our names; Laureano's surname was Bueno Hermosa, good and beautiful.'

Coming out of the Church

She looked at her husband and laughed.

'Well then we moved to Málaga, where my husband had a business that made jute sacks for a company that had an arrangement with Pakistan to import the jute, but did not have the means to make the sacks. My sister-in-law had got married the year before and my father-in-law had bought a house for them in Málaga; they lived in a flat on the first floor. It was an old house and my father-in-law had two more floors constructed, one for us and one for his other son, who was a doctor. We lived there for thirty years until the day when we decided to buy a washing machine. There was a terrace where we did the washing and hung the clothes out to dry, but it was impossible to get the new washing machine up the stairs; there were no lifts. So we decided to move to a house near the Plaza del Teatro. Then my sister-in-law bought a house next door to us, then my brother-in-law as well. So I lived next door to my brother and sister-in-law almost all my married life.

Not long after we were married our son Alberto was born, then a few years later we had a daughter, Mary Loly.'

At this point her daughter came in from the kitchen carrying a tray with a pot of tea for one and a huge plate of cakes. She began to pour me some tea.

'Is no-one else having tea?' I asked.

'No, this is for you. We will be having dinner soon.'

'So, Lola, when you think back over your life what strikes you as being particularly different from the life of your own daughter?' I asked, sipping the hot tea.

She paused and thought for a moment, then looked at her husband.

'I was always very happy with my life,' she said. 'I had a wonderful life. But looking back now I think I would have liked to have had a job. I would have liked to have worked and had my own money, to have been a bit more independent.'

Later, as I was about to leave she stood up and said:

'Wait a minute, I have something for you.'

A few minutes later she returned with a glass jar wrapped in a paper bag.

'This is a speciality from Rio Gordo,' she explained. *'Caracoles en caldillo.'*

'Snails in a wonderful stock,' her son explained. 'Rio Gordo is famous for its snails.'

It turned out that each year, in May, the people of Rio Gordo celebrate the "Day of the Snail" and people come from far and wide to taste the *caracoles*. In some years as many as two thousand people will descend on the village, where some 50,000 snails will have been cleaned and cooked for the festivities. For over forty years the villagers have been holding snail tastings, setting up their stalls on the edge of the village, and then in 1999 they decided to make it an official day.

Apparently the best time to collect the snails is when there is no wind, no sun and it is raining. There are two types of snail that can be found in Rio Gordo: *el caracol del terrano*, which is the whiter one and is more popular, and *el caracol boyuno*, which has a dark shell. The locals admit that the snails have very little flavour and insist that it is the stock that makes the Rio Gordo snails so special. It is a long process to prepare the snails. First of all they are left in water for two weeks to clean them thoroughly then they are washed with water and vinegar. Next the liquid is skimmed to remove the scum and the snails are put in warm water so that they emerge from their shells, then the heat is turned up to cook them. All that remains to do next is add the herbs and spices. The traditional Rio Gordo recipe contains:

Dried orange peel
Black pepper
Aniseed
Mint
Basil
A sprig of rosemary
Chili
Salt

Occasionally they add rice, but the traditional method is with just the stock. The snails are usually eaten in May and August, neither month renowned for its rain, so that may explain why they are so expensive. Local people say that nowadays they can sell a kilo of snails for seven euros.

Latafundia

Lola's village was not a typical example; a village with five millers was a profitable one. Despite the mountains that surrounded it the land was fertile and level and wheat grew well. However much of Spain, and in particular Andalucia, was subject to the system of latafundia and whilst the landlords held thousands of acres of fertile land, the peasants were crowded onto areas of poor, stony soil where it was difficult to grow anything except olives or pasture a few goats. According to the historian Max Gallo, 200,000 landowners owned 40% of all cultivated land whilst three million peasants were landless. It was typical to find a large estate, often uncultivated, with great swathes of land given over to private hunting or the breeding of horses and fighting bulls, alongside a number of small plots of unproductive land which were insufficient to support a family and others rented from the landowner on a short term lease by a few small farmers. The peasants were not only at the mercy of their landlord and the money lender, but also of the climate; a long period of drought could devastate the region.

In 1935 the geographer E.H.G. Doby recalled that a woman who worked on an Andalusian pig farm had taken him to see her home, remarking that it was worse than the pigs' sty. The conditions were so foul that he had had to agree with her, but reported that the owners' response had been no more than: "You have a roof over your head. What more do you want?"

MARIA MATHILDE born in Málaga 1946

Maria Mathilde is married and has no children. She was born in Málaga and has lived there all her life. She and her sister owned and ran a clothing store in the city centre until she married. She no longer goes to work. She not only gave an account of her own life but also of her mother and grandmothers' lives.

Maria is a friend from the golf club. One day after a particularly enjoyable game of golf in the autumn sunshine, we were sitting in the clubhouse having lunch and discussing the highs and lows of our game, when she said she had to leave early because her mother was unwell and she wanted to visit her.

'Does she live in Málaga?' I asked.

'Yes, but she was born in Almeria,' she replied and then began to tell me about her and her grandmother.

Seeing my interest she said:

'Look, why don't you come round tomorrow for *merienda*, afternoon tea, and I'll tell you all about her.'

The next afternoon I presented myself at her modern town house bordering the golf course. She greeted me affectionately and led me into the lounge. The table was already set with cups and a plate of biscuits.

'The tea will just be a minute,' she said. 'Then we can get started.'

I sat down on the sofa and waited. Sure enough after a moment she returned carrying two cups of herbal tea.

'Right, where should I begin?' she asked.

'Well your grandmother sounded a very interesting lady,' I replied. 'Why not start with her.'

'Good idea. My grandparents are all dead now, but my maternal grandmother lived with us for many years, so I remember her very well.'

HIPOLITE born in Berja 1876-1958

'My maternal grandmother, Hipolite was a woman who had lots of stories to tell and I loved to listen to her; I learnt a lot from her. When I was about four years old she became bedridden. She had a fever, which they treated with some kind of injection, but they made a mistake and instead of injecting her intravenously, they injected into the muscle and her leg became infected. It took a long time to heal and all that time she was unable to walk; she was a big woman, tall and strong, not fat but corpulent and by the time the leg had healed, she found that she couldn't walk any more. Of course there was no physiotherapy then and nobody suggested she exercise her muscles. In fact she never walked again; she was disabled for eight years, until she died aged eighty-two.

My parents gave my grandmother the main living room, right by the front door, with her own bedroom and a bathroom alongside; that was her world. Each morning my mother would help her out of bed and into an armchair, and there she would stay all day. Nobody had wheelchairs in those days. I remember her sitting in that chair; she was always dressed in a white blouse with rows of smocking across the top and a large, black and white apron that covered her black skirt. I don't remember seeing her ever wear anything else. She was like a queen holding court: family, neighbours, friends, everyone would visit her. She would give people advice on all sorts of things, and she had a way of making their problems seem less important, less difficult to sort out. Despite her disability she was a very positive woman and she was always doing something. She loved to crochet and if she found out that a neighbour or a friend was expecting a baby she would send my mother out to buy some wool so that she could make something for them. She was very clever at sewing, repairing all our clothes and even making us new things out of old material; anyone that needed something altered would come along and see my grandmother.

She had a friend, Maria, whose husband owned a grocery shop and every afternoon Maria would come to visit her. She sat in the living room with my grandmother and told her about the films she had seen or recounted the radio soap-operas that she had been listening to. There was no television then and my grandmother was a bit deaf, so she didn't listen to the radio much, but she loved to listen to her friend's stories.'

At this point Maria stopped and laughed.

'That woman saw all the latest films but she never once paid to go to the cinema. Do you know what she did? Well she would take a group of us kids to see a film; we would all pay and go into the cinema and she would go off and do some shopping. Then a bit later she would come back and say to the man in the ticket office: "Alright if I just take a look to see how the children are?" Of course he always said yes and then she would join us. Even if we had seen it all we would watch the film a second time round, so that she could see it too.

She was a very kind woman, but I always thought she was a bit strange, because her hair was tightly permed and she wore lots of make-up and very strong perfume. She looked quite different to the other women that came to our house.

My grandmother had a very lively mind and she liked to read the newspaper every day. It was called "*La España*" and she also liked a magazine called "*Regesdes*". Before my father came home at midday, she would call my mother and tell her to fold the paper carefully, so that it was not creased and put it back in its place ready for him to read.

I never remember hearing her complain. In fact it was just the opposite; if my mother had to go out or do something, she would always say: "Don't you worry about me, Mati; I'll be fine until you get back."

My grandmother was born in Berja, a village near Almeria, in the Sierra de Gádo, in 1876. When she was about fifteen, my grandfather, Tomás, proposed to her, but she considered him too old for her and turned him down. I think he was probably ten or twelve years older than her. So anyway he decided to leave the village and emigrate to Argentina, where he worked for more than fifteen years. He must have had a number of jobs, but his last job is the one we know about, when he was a cook for the President of Argentina. He obviously never forgot my grandmother, because he came back to the village and proposed again. This time she must have viewed him differently: a man who'd travelled and who had money. Also she was older herself by then and saw life differently. So when she was thirty-two they got married. They had six children, though only three survived. My mother was the youngest and she told me how she always thought of her parents as being very old, which I suppose they were; after all, my grandmother was forty-five when my mother was born.

My grandparents were very happy together; they were very close in everything they did. They lived a comfortable life in Berja; the money my grandfather had earned in Argentina made them quite well off by local standards. He used the money to start a business in the middle of the village; he rented a house in the central square and opened a bodega and a pawn shop. He didn't want his children to end up working in the fields, like the other local children.

Hipolite's daughter Mati

My grandmother took a job helping the local schoolteacher; she was not qualified, but she was a very intelligent woman and when the teacher left, she took over the school. Normally the children stayed in school until they were ten or twelve, unless of course they had to work in the fields or at home, in which case they left when they were eight. People with money kept their children at school longer and then sent them away to Granada or Madrid to finish their studies. My mother didn't go away to school, but she didn't have to work either. She was almost twenty before she had to work, and that was through a change in their circumstances.

Although he had worked as a cook in Argentina, my grandfather never once cooked at home, but he was very strict about certain things: everyone had to sit down at the table to eat at the same time, the table had to be set nicely with a table cloth and cutlery and there was always to be a bowl of fresh fruit on the sideboard. He wanted mealtimes to be a kind of ceremony. This was not at all usual in the villages, where generally people ate very informally, grabbing something to eat as soon as they came in from the fields.

I don't remember my grandfather at all; he died before I was born, but my mother always describes him as a very honourable man and very affectionate. He was not like the other men in the village; he dressed differently, behaved differently. It was probably the influence of living in a big city in Argentina for so long.

Then the Civil War came and for some reason, which I have never really understood because Berja was not affected very much by the war, my grandfather was evicted from his house in the village square and had to close down his businesses. The family had nowhere to live and not much money, so it was hard for them. My grandfather had not been a very good businessman; he had earned what he needed and no more, and he had spent it making sure his family were well cared for, instead of investing or saving any money. Anyway he would not stay in the village after that; he had too much pride. So my grandparents moved to Granada. By then they were both quite old so they took my mother with them to look after them.

Things were pretty awful for them in Granada; they rented some rooms in an old house in a poor part of the town and lived as best they could. They had no real means of earning a livelihood, so my grandmother who was always very resourceful, cut up the old clothes and bits of material that she had and made new clothes from them. But people in Granada were not interested in buying clothes; they were more interested in survival. So she packed a suitcase with these clothes and set off in a rickety old bus to sell them in the villages of the Alpujarra. The Alpujarra is a mountainous area near Granada, dotted with tiny villages that are linked by twisting, narrow roads. The people that lived there hardly ever came into the city. It was very dangerous to travel anywhere then because you could be shot by the troops of either side, but my grandmother was a strong woman and very brave. She said she would be fine because the people of the Apujarra were different; they were open-hearted and generous, and also very united: there were not the splits in families between Nationalists and Republicans that you found elsewhere. Her clothes were very popular with the people of these remote mountain villages and as nobody had any money to buy them, she learnt to barter. Each trip she returned home with her suitcase full of produce: pieces of smoked ham, goats' cheese, coffee, chickpeas, fruit, sausages, honey and sometimes even a few pesetas. Actually money was of little use in Granada because there was no food in the shops to buy. Anyway, thanks to her efforts, the family never went hungry.'

Women in the Civil War

One of the key issues at stake in the Civil War, although rarely stated explicitly, was the future position of women. When the war ended in 1939 and Franco revoked all the gains awarded to women by the Second Republic some were relieved to return to their traditional role and others were forced to accept the situation or go into exile, to prison or to the firing squad.

Even the way women dressed was an issue during wartime. In the Republican areas bourgeois dress, especially the wearing of hats, was seen as incriminating. Going bareheaded represented solidarity and was akin to making a gender statement. In the early days of the war many young Republican women started to dress in unisex dungarees, referred to as "monos". This mode of dress lasted no more than a year, possibly because of its connotations with the Communist party. It was replaced by the practical wearing of culottes and sturdy shoes, ideal for the jobs Republican women found themselves doing: clearing up rubble, working in the fields, riding bicycles.

At the outbreak of war women as well as men rushed to defend their cities; they wanted to be soldiers too. A "Times" correspondent wrote at the time of armed and aggressive milita-women standing alongside men at the front-line. He complained that all that womanhood traditionally stood for was disappearing.

The most voluble woman on the Republican side was Dolores Ibárruri, known as La Pasionaria. She was a Communist and a prominent member of "Women against War and Fascism". She is particularly remembered for her radio broadcast on 19th July 1936 when she appealed to the Spanish people to stand up and oppose fascism, using the phrase for which she is best remembered " ¿No pasarán!", "They shall not pass". She rallied both men and women to the Republican cause with her impassioned speeches and energetic campaigning. At the end of the war she fled into exile in the USSR and did not return to Spain until the death of Franco in 1975.

Although no other Republican woman at the time held such an influential position many young women found themselves in positions of responsibility: organising food supplies, running evening classes, writing articles and giving speeches for the war effort.

However despite the new freedom experienced by some women during the war, many others found that their husbands' attitudes had not changed. They were still expected to produce the meals on time and were not allowed to join political parties. Dolores Ibárruri said that when she asked her comrades why they did not bring their wives to the meetings, the reply was that their women did not understand politics, that they had to stay at home to look after the children. Even when women went to the front line to fight they were still expected to exchange their gun for a broom when necessary.

MATI born in Berja in 1921

'What about your mother?' I asked Mari next.

'My grandmother always called my mother Mati, but her name was actually Matilde, the same as mine. Mati had a good childhood, my grandmother made sure that she had an education and she never had to work, not even in the house. So when they moved to Granada I think she found it rather hard. She got a job as a maid in the house of a lawyer and his family. They were very good to her, but it was not what she was accustomed to, and although there were two other maids, she was the youngest and had to do the hardest work. She suffered from chilblains in the cold winters and her soft hands were soon covered in blisters.

Conditions in Granada were crowded; sanitation was poor and there was no food, so it was not surprising that not long after they had moved to the city there was an outbreak of typhus, which the local people called the "*Piojo Verde*". This was still a few years before there was a reliable vaccine and their only method of controlling the epidemic was to isolate people in the fever hospitals, where they inevitably died. There were hundreds of deaths that year. When my mother became sick with the "*Piojo Verde*" my grandparents were very worried. They thought she would die and then they would be left without anyone to look after them, but my mother was very fortunate. Her employers refused to let them take her away to St. Lazarus, the quarantine hospital; they washed her and shaved her head to remove the lice and put her to bed in a room in the attic, where they looked after her night and day until she recovered. They were very kind people; they knew how much her parents relied on her.

After she left and got married she still kept in touch with them. They became very good friends, went to her wedding and were god-parents to her children. When I was a young girl I remember meeting them a few times when they came to visit us in Málaga.

When my mother was in Granada she used to write to my father regularly. She had met him when the war had broken out and he had been sent to her village with the *Guardia de Asalto*, the security police established by the Republican government to keep public order. She was twenty at the time. The villagers in Berja were both Nationalists and Republicans, but there was never any fighting there. If any soldiers went through the village my grandfather would make my mother stay inside in case there was any trouble, but there never was. There was only one death during the entire war and that was an accident: one of the local women was cleaning the barracks one day when a soldier, accidently fired his gun and killed her. If my grandparents had stayed in their village during the war instead of going to Granada they would not have suffered such hardship.

In my father's village it was very different. He was born in Cañete La Real, not far from Ronda in the province of Málaga. My father was the youngest of six children and the only way his father could afford to educate him was to send him away to the seminary in Cádiz to study to become a priest. My father hated it there and after a few years he decided to escape in a lorry that was transporting melons to Málaga. He never became a priest but he did have a better education than his brothers and he could type, a skill which later became very useful.

When the invading forces, the Italians, the Nationalist army and the Moroccan regular soldiers advanced on Málaga they did so via the mountains of Ronda and my father's village. The soldiers devastated Cañete La Real; they tortured and killed many people. My aunt told me how the soldiers would force the women to drink castor oil until they vomited so that they would tell them where their men were hiding. One night the soldiers came and shot my grandfather, who was in his seventies, two of his sons and his two sons-in-law. Luckily my father had already been called up by the Republicans and was in Alicante, and his other brother was away fighting in the war at the time, or they would all have been shot. There were a lot of divisions in that village: people fighting amongst themselves, families split in their allegiances.

When the war broke out my father was still very young and hadn't done his military service, but they were mobilising all men over fifteen. As I said my father was well educated, so very soon after he was called up they transferred him to Alicante to work in the Civil Government. He was still there when the city fell in April 1939, the last Republican city to fall into Nationalist hands. He was imprisoned in a concentration camp in Albatera in Murcia for two months. He and the other prisoners really suffered in there; there was hardly any food, they had to eat potato peelings and orange peel. When they were given some food it was only ever hard bread and water. At night the local villagers would creep up to the fence and throw over some bread or whatever they could spare to help them. According to my aunt my father once went for twenty-five days without any food. It was a very frightening experience for him because every day the soldiers would take some of the prisoners out and shoot them. Then he had a real stroke of luck: a friend of his, who had worked with him in Alicante, had managed to evade arrest and was working in the government offices in Málaga. He arranged for him to be transferred to the prison in Málaga.

This kind action probably saved his life, because nobody ever survived the concentration camps.

When he arrived in Málaga he soon got to know people in the prison and someone gave him a newspaper on Socialism; from then on until his death he was a staunch Socialist. He used to hide this Socialist newspaper under his mattress and one night when the guards read out the list for the next day, his name was on it. He thought that they had found out about the newspaper and that he was going to be shot. Usually the list contained the names of those invited to go on the *pasarela,* a joking reference to the long walk to the firing squad. He passed a very miserable night, worrying about his mother and sister and who would care for them if he was shot, thinking about my mother who was still writing to him from Granada and convinced that this was to be his last night. When morning came he was taken out by the guard to an office and there was his friend, Pepe Poso; he had wangled a job for him in the government office where he worked. I'm not sure how he managed it because everything was in the control of the Nationalists by then, but anyway you can imagine my father's relief.

He worked there for a while and when he was able, left to find another job outside of the government. He rented a small house in Victoria Street in the centre of Málaga and sent for his widowed sister to look after him. As soon as the house was ready he went to Granada for my mother, who was twenty-one by then and he was twenty-three. They married and he brought her to Málaga to live. He never spoke of his experiences to me or to my sister, not because it was painful for him, but because we lived in a time of repression, and he didn't want to influence us in any way that would put us in danger. He wanted to protect us from his beliefs because for years after the war people were still being arrested and shot for saying the wrong things. My mother wasn't ever interested in politics; she just went along with whatever my father said, and she never spoke much about the war either; I learnt most from my aunt.

Mati and her husband

El Piojo Verde

There are various strains of typhus, but the one which was colloquially known in Spain as "el piojo verde" was certainly epidemic typhus. It was sometimes called "jail fever" or "famine fever" because it occurred whenever there were low standards of hygiene and poverty and very often after or during wars.

The disease itself was endemic in rats and mice and the bacteria were spread to humans through lice, fleas or mites from these creatures. Lice biting an infected person would then go on to bite someone else and spread the disease.

The symptoms usually appeared very quickly and were severe: headaches, high fevers, coughs, rashes, muscle pains, chills, delirium and stupor. It was the last symptom that gave rise to its name, from the Greek word "typhos" which means dozey or lazy.

Nowadays the infection is treated with antibiotics and can be controlled if the treatment is started in time. When Mati had the "Piojo Verde" there was no vaccine and there were no antibiotics available in Granada; the disease had to run its course, hence the importance of quarantine.

A safe vaccine was developed in 1938 and was widely used during World War II, since when such epidemics have been eradicated in Europe. Improved standards of hygiene and the use of DDT to kill the lice have also helped to reduce the occurrence of epidemic typhus.

ANA born in Cañete la Real

'What about your father's mother? Did you ever meet her?' I asked.

'I don't remember much about Ana, my paternal grandmother. She was a very unhappy woman and always dressed in black. Now looking back on it, I think she was very depressed. My father was very good to her: when he bought a bigger house with a garden for my mother and us, he brought his mother to Málaga to live in the house in Victoria Street with his sister.

When my parents married my father took his bride back to his village to meet my grandmother. She didn't like my mother; she thought she wasn't the right one for her son. It's funny you know because my mother is a very quiet woman, but when she visited his village everyone thought my father had married an actress because she wore fancy clothes: a narrow skirt and fitted blouse, nylon stockings, high heeled shoes and make-up. Nothing unusual in Málaga, but in Cañete La Real the women were still wearing long, black skirts and black shawls; the whole village was in mourning, even the children. They all considered her a bit strange at first, but once they got to know her and saw how kind she was, they changed their opinions.

My father brought all his surviving family to Málaga and looked after them, even helping his nephews find work. And of course my mother helped him with that.

My mother hated visiting my father's village; it was so primitive. There was no source of water; the only water came from a standpipe between the hours of five am and nine am each day. The villagers would form a queue with their clay, water containers, *cantaros*, the night before, and leave a long line of these pots stretched along the street. My mother told me how one night, when the fair was there, a fairground lorry came along the street in the dark and, not seeing the pots, broke them all one by one. The sound was like gunfire and terrified the villagers; they thought the war had started again.

There was no bathroom in my grandmother's house; the toilet was outside, a hole in the ground behind a large rock and there was a small sink in the bedroom. My mother would tell me how she would not be able to go to the toilet all the time she was there; there was always someone walking past the rock or the goats would wander up and disturb her. She hated it there.

Even when I visited the village in the late fifties, I was about thirteen years old at the time, there were no water, no gas and no telephone. There was some electricity, but it was very weak. The kitchen was small and dark, and at one end there was an open hearth with a very primitive stove; everything was cooked with wood or charcoal. If the villagers wanted to go to the town there was only a very old car that acted as public transport; it was always breaking down because it had overheated and steam would pour out of the front.

Before the soldiers shot her husband and her sons my grandmother had a fairly comfortable life. My grandfather had had a gang of sixteen or seventeen men that he would take to local towns looking for work. They would help with the harvest or construction, whatever work they could get. Sometimes they went as far as Seville to find work. But with her husband dead and her sons living away from home life had become very hard for my grandmother so it's not surprising that I don't remember her smiling much.'

At this point, Maria got up and stretched.

'I don't know about you, but I could do with some more tea. All this talking is making me thirsty.'

I followed her out to her kitchen, a large, airy modern room very unlike the one she had just been describing. She took a packet of herbal tea from the cupboard and began to brew a strong infusion with it.

'Very good for the blood,' she explained. 'Do you want some honey in it?'

Maria was a good-looking woman, always smartly dressed, but never glamorous. Her blonde hair was stylishly cut and swept across her forehead and her make-up was immaculate.

'Why don't you tell me something about your own life now,' I suggested as we walked back to the terrace, carrying the tea tray.

From our seats on the terrace we could watch the golfers playing the sixteenth hole. It was peaceful, the summer air filled with the noise of the cicadas and broken only by the occasional sound of a golf ball being struck.

Women's Rights

Although there was no great feminist movement in Spain in the 1960s and 70s as there was in other countries the beginning of the century had its share of feminist thinkers. At that time education for middle and upper-class women began to improve. Women began to fight to break the "iron ceiling". In 1915 the Residencia de Señoritas opened in Madrid. Most of the women who stayed there were training to be teachers; one of them, María Goyri, was one of the first women in Spain to receive her doctorate. In 1918 the co-educational Instituto Escuela opened with the mandate to widen the range of people's studies. Then in 1920 the Academia de Jurisprudencia opened its doors to women and women began to train as lawyers.

The Asociacíon de Mujeres Españolas (Association of Spanish Women) was established and organised by women of the right-wing aristocracy but it still dealt with very liberal issues such as abortion, the right of women to have jobs in the universities and on the tribunals, salary rights and subsidies for the publication of women's literature. Then in 1926 María Maeztu, the founder of the Residencia de Señoritas, opened the Lyceum Club Feminino in Madrid. Despite the misogynist protests at the time it became a cultural centre for women to meet and exchange ideas.

In 1925 María Cambrils, a Socialist from Valencia published a book on the freedom of women and in 1927 Margarita Nelken published "En torno a nosotros" about the equality of the sexes. Women were beginning not just to think about equality but to talk and write about it. With the establishment of the Republic in 1931 women redoubled their efforts to have some changes made. They had the vote and now they made inroads into government. Federica Montseny was named Minister of Health in 1936, the first woman in the world to have a ministerial appointment at that time. More women became involved in politics. This was the period when Dolores Ibárruri, "La Pasionaria" arrived in Madrid as a spokeswoman for the Communist Party and Irene Falcón founded the organisation "Mujeres Antifascistas" (Antifascist Women) which was 50,000 strong. In 1936 Matilde de la Torre became a congress-woman for the Popluar Front during their short period of their government. But it was not easy for women in politics because there was so much resistance from men. The women were the butt of jokes in Parliament and they were under constant scrutiny in both their public and personal lives, especially those who did not have a "normal" life, that is a husband and children. But by 1939 all the reforms that were made during that period had been annulled and many of these intellectual women were banished into exile and oblivion as the Republic fell and Franco took power. The women of Spain had lost two wars: the Civil War and the war of their sex.

"Mujeres Libres"

During the early part of the century a number of women's organisations were formed. The most important of these was "Mujeres Libres", "Free Women", which was founded in May 1936. These women did not consider themselves as feminists, rather they saw themselves as trying to get women directly involved in the struggle for liberation; freeing women from the domination of men was only the first step in freeing everyone from all kinds of domination. "Mujeres Libres" existed for only two years but during that time it had over 30,000 women members. The main focus was on education and they opened schools for women, running technical courses to prepare women to work in industry and teaching them to fight for equal rights in the workplace; they gave them military training and taught them how to shoot; they opened maternity hospitals; they provided schools for young children and set up child care centres for workers' children. In 1937 they opened the Casa de la Dona, a major women's college in Barcelona, which by the following year had an intake of between six and eight hundred women a day. "Mujeres Libres" were instrumental in getting the government of the Second Republic to change the law on abortion, contraception and divorce. Many other groups were formed as part of Communist or Socialists groups, but never became anything more than "women's sections". Only "Mujeres Libres" took women's emancipation seriously; they believed that if the domination of women ended then all types of domination would end.

However when women's legal rights were eventually restored it was not as part of a feminist movement but as part of a wider movement for democracy. The new constitution of 1978 defined equality in the following words:

"The Spanish are equal in the eyes of the law, and no discrimination by birth, race, sex, religion, opinion or any other condition or circumstance, private or social can prevail." (Art. 14 CE)

There was no longer any official state religion, the voting age was established at eighteen for men and women, but divorce and abortion were still forbidden.

MARIA MATHILDE

'My sister, Ana, and I were born in the house in Victoria Street; she is two years older than me. When I was four my father bought a *casa mata*, that's what they called detached houses with gardens in those days, near the Hospital Civil. It was a lovely house with an interior patio, a big garden, a fountain and lots of space. It was what you might call a middle-class area; our new neighbours were doctors and lawyers. At the time I felt we had moved right out of the city because we had to cross the bridge to get back to the centre, but in actual fact it was probably only a couple of kilometres from our old house. I lived there until I got married.

When we moved to the *casa mata* my mother brought my grandmother Hipolite from Granada to live with us because by then my grandfather, Tomás had died. My memories of my childhood are very happy ones; there was always a relaxed atmosphere in our house. My mother was very laid-back and content with her life; she wasn't as intelligent as my grandmother, nor as positive a character, but she was always smiling. She still is; I always think of her with a smile on her face.

Lots of our neighbours' children went to religious schools, but my father didn't want me to go to one, even though there was a convent almost next door, so I went to the local school until I was thirteen. My father had always wanted his daughters to be independent. He rented a clothes shop in the centre of the city so that my sister and I could work there. It was in an old *barrio,* a working-class district, and he opened a loan shop next door to it, so he could give credit to the people who wanted to buy things in the shop. It worked very well; if someone needed to buy clothes for a wedding for example, he would lend them the money and they would come to us to buy them. I used to do all the accounts and my sister bought the clothes, and we both served in the shop. I didn't really like working there at first because I was very shy and didn't like talking to the customers, but after a while I got used to it. Sometimes I would go with my father, riding on the back of his scooter, to visit other shops that he did business with.

My father was always very interested in me; he liked to teach me things: how to drive, how to play the guitar, how to type. One day he offered to buy me a car, but I said no. It would have meant I would have needed a driving licence and to get that I had to do six months social service, like my sister had. So I said I would prefer a guitar instead; he went to a local guitar maker and had one made especially for me. He even took me to watch them making it and then he sent me to Flamenco guitar lessons. I didn't really learn a lot, because Flamenco guitar is really only about accompaniment, but I did learn to appreciate Flamenco music. At that time it was considered a bit low-class, and not really appreciated as it is today, but my father loved it and whenever we went out he would take the first opportunity to sing it.

He was always looking for ways to teach us something; he was very concerned that we should become good citizens and good parents. If I had a bad school report he would go to see the teacher or even hire a private tutor for me, because that was what he considered a good parent would do. Although my father was not religious he made us take our first communion because all the other children at school were doing it and he didn't want us to look odd.

My mother was different; she was like a hen, clucking about:

"*Nena*, set the table for your father. *Nena* do this or that or I'll tell your father and he'll be cross with you."

My father remained a Socialist all his life, although that was something he did not talk to us about; he wanted to protect us. He was very well known in the *barrio* and helped lots of people when they had problems or were sick. People looked to him as their representative; he was involved in everything and had lots of friends. I think some of them thought of him as rich because he had his own car and a house. He was always out, either working or talking politics with his friends, and even when he retired he was still out every day. It was as though my parents led two completely separate lives; my mother never went out with him, she stayed at home alone. I don't think they had a very happy marriage, but my mother never complained. I expect she had got used to it.'

Maria paused and drank some of her tea.

'Tell me about how you met your husband,' I said.

'Well Manolo's mother owned a shoe shop not far from our shop and my father knew him. In fact I had seen him once or twice on my visits with my father, but I wasn't really interested in boys, not like my sister. Then one day my sister introduced us; she knew all the boys in the area. It wasn't love at first sight, but I liked his type, so we began to go out together. Shortly afterwards his father decided to go to France to work and Manolo went with him, but he wrote to me all the time. Then he received his call-up papers and he had to either come back to Spain and do two years military service or stay in France for good, so he came home. That meant two more years of letters before he was discharged and could look for work. Even when he found a job he wouldn't marry me until he had brought all of his family back from France: his parents and his sister. By the time he had everyone settled he was twenty-nine and I was twenty-seven and then we got married.

My father was not keen for me to get married; he wanted me to have my own life and not live in the shadow of a husband. He wanted me to be independent and responsible for my own life. The only bout of depression I remember my father ever having was when he knew I was getting married.

I suppose I upset my father's plans a bit because I didn't want to continue working in the shop. I felt I had spent enough of my life there; I had worked there for fourteen years, from nine in the morning until two in the afternoon and again from four until ten at night, every day except Sunday, even *fiestas*. I just didn't want to continue; I had never much liked it anyway. My sister continued with it, and still runs it now. I told my father I would help out from time to time if he needed me, but that I wanted to live my own life. I have never worked since and to be honest I have never missed it. Manolo's working hours have always been irregular, so if I worked we probably wouldn't see much of each other. I had hoped that when we got married we would have some children, like my sister, but we never did. We do enjoy our nieces and nephews though; they are our family now, especially little Mario.'

She smiled with pleasure. I knew how much she loved her niece's new baby, born only a few months earlier.

'Anyway,' she continued. 'I have a very full life: I play golf, sometimes I paint, I play the organ and I do yoga, and of course I look after the house and Manolo. Life with Manolo is never dull; he is always trying new things, especially things with a spiritual or supernatural connection. Over the years we have learnt about UFOs, numerology, astrology, occult sciences, colours, crystals; we have studied Buddhism, the

Koran, philosophy and we even became good friends with a guru. He was a lovely man who died very young; a group of us would meet at his house and discuss philosophy every week. Manolo wants to try everything and I am happy to go along with him; we even celebrated Mass in our home at one time and we used to go to English classes.'

She laughed when she saw the expression on my face; I had never heard either one of them speak a word of English.

'You know he is always picking up strays,' she said, with a slightly exasperated look on her face. 'One day, not long after we moved here, I was in the kitchen, preparing lunch, when I heard Manolo calling me.

"Mari, come and see what I've got for you."

I said: "Not another cat or dog, Manolo, we just don't have any room for them."

"No, no, come and see."

When I opened the door to let him in there was a young Arab boy standing next to him; he was about my height, very thin and very brown skinned. He must have been thirteen or fourteen years old.

"He's going to stay with us until we can find his brother," Manolo said. "What's for lunch?"

Eventually I got the whole story out of him. Manolo had been having a drink in the bar at the golf club, when some of the children that play there had come in asking for money. When the men asked what they wanted the money for, they said to buy a sandwich for a boy who was lost. The other men were just going to give them the money, but of course Manolo wanted to see who this lost boy was.

The boy was an illegal immigrant who had come across from Morocco by clinging to the underside of a lorry that was returning to Málaga. He could not speak Spanish but had a piece of paper with a few useful phrases written on it. That's how we discovered that he was trying to reach his brother who worked in Barcelona, but the only information he had was his brother's name and the village where he lived.

I couldn't see how we could help him. Our friends all said that we shouldn't get involved; if the police found out we would be in trouble for helping an illegal immigrant. But Manolo wouldn't listen to anyone. There was a company in Barcelona that he had worked with for years, so he rang the director, who was a friend of his and asked him to trace the boy's brother. It took a little while but he did it and gave the brother our number so that he could telephone us.

In the meantime the boy lived with us. At first he was very scared and wouldn't speak or do anything, but after a few days when he realised that we were planning to send him to his brother he changed completely, laughing and smiling and making himself quite at home. I bought him some clothes of course and gave him the spare room to sleep in. He was always a bit shy of me but would follow Manolo around as if they were joined at the hip; he seemed to worship him.

It took a little while to organise his journey; we had the problem of how to get him there without the police catching him. He had no papers so we couldn't send him by air, nor on a bus; the only way was by train. So we booked him a sleeper compartment, direct from Málaga to Barcelona, bought him a Walkman, so that he could listen to music and not speak to anyone, and gave him some food and money for the journey. We were very worried he would be discovered, but everything worked out alright and his brother met him at Barcelona station as planned.'

'Do you still hear from him?' I asked.

'No, we never heard any more,' she said.

She smiled and repeated:

'Anyway, as you can see, life with Manolo is never dull.'

Illegal immigrants

In 2004 there were 3.69 million foreigners in Spain, more than eight percent of a population of 44,000,000. At least 700,000 of them were illegal and working in the 'black' economy. So the Government decided to offer an amnesty to those that could produce a work contract and proof that they had lived in the country for more than six months. It had advantages all round - security for the immigrants and payments into the State purse in terms of taxes and social security contributions.

It was estimated by the Spanish government that over 800,000 illegal immigrants arrived in Spain, in 2005 alone. Most of them arrived in boats and landed on the south coast of Andalusia, some crossed the border into Ceuta and Melilla, others landed in the Canary Islands. Most of them arrived penniless, without identity papers and often with health problems. Sometimes the journey was too hard and their craft too fragile and they were drowned, their dead bodies washed up on the beaches of the Costa del Sol for the police to recover. The lucky ones made their way up towards Almeria and got jobs picking fruit and vegetables, others found casual work in the construction industry and some drifted into crime and prostitution.

By 2012, in a bid to reduce the budget deficit, the Government decided to withold free health care from all illegal immigrants. This is currently being disputed by the Council of Europe as being illegal under the EU Social Charter.

LETICIA born in Germany in 1961

Leticia was born in Germany in 1961; she is married and has four children but recently she and her husband decided to separate. She works as a singer, song-writer and musician, has recorded numerous CDs, some of which she has posted on You Tube, and has own group. Her mother is French and her father Spanish. She has lived in New York, went to university in the United States and speaks fluent English. Since returning to Spain she has lived in Madrid, Ronda and now lives in Velez Málaga.

I owned one of Leticia's CDs; I had bought it when we heard her sing at a friend's party the previous summer. I remember my first impression was of a slender young woman wearing a scarlet shawl; she wandered amongst the guests singing a Spanish folksong, with the castanets in her hands rippling in time.

'This is the woman,' she said holding up the castanet in her right hand, making it chatter rapidly. 'And this is the man.' The castanet in her left hand clacked brusquely. The audience laughed; they had warmed to her immediately.

When I had telephoned her to arrange our meeting she had sounded very interested in the book and keen to talk to me, so I had arranged to meet her outside her flat at six o'clock the next Sunday. As usual I was early but did not have to wait long before I saw her walking up the road towards me. She was a tall, slim woman, with long, brown hair and a face that sparkled with life.

'Have you been waiting long?' she asked, searching in her bag for her keys.

'A few minutes only,' I replied.

'The children are at home; I think it would be better if we went to the park to talk,' she said. 'But maybe you'd like to come in first and meet my mother. I have to go up and speak to her anyway; I've been out all afternoon.'

We climbed a dingy, narrow staircase until we reached the second floor. She unlocked the door and invited me to go inside. One of her daughters came to greet us, closely followed by her mother, a tall woman in her early seventies with long grey hair, tied back in a ponytail.

'Shall we have some tea?' she asked Leticia. 'I'll go and get some cakes if you like.'

Later as we sat around the table drinking herbal tea and eating some rather sticky cakes, bought from the nearby bakery, Leticia explained that her mother was actually French but had lived in Spain since she was eighteen. Her name was Jeanette and she had come to Spain to study, fell in love and stayed.

'I was a Communist,' Jeannette confessed with a wry grin, 'living in Franco's Spain.'

'My mother has had an interesting life, maybe you would like to hear a little about it while we finish our tea?' Leticia suggested.

I nodded, my mouth full of cake.

Her mother began:

'Well I do have something interesting to tell you; something that affected my whole life. I met my husband, Leticia's father, not long after I came to Spain. He was very good looking and from a well-off family. He worked for his father, who owned a lot of shops, as his comercial representative. The family was very well known in Málaga and they did not think much of him going out with me, a foreigner and a Communist, but we were in love and so continued to see each other. When we decided to get married the family was very much against it so we ran away to France and got married in Paris. We stayed abroad for quite a few years, travelling all over Europe. Leticia was born in Germany and her sister was born in Switzerland. Later on I had two other children, both born in Málaga.

Well after our second child was born we decided to return to Málaga. That was when everything started to go wrong. It was in the 1960s. We lived in Torremolinos and my husband began to go out every night without me; he had a different woman each night, all foreigners; he liked foreigners. By then I had three children and was busy looking after them and running the home, but life was becoming impossible for me. In those days we were unable to divorce so we separated and it was while we were living apart that I met someone else and I had another child.'

At this point Leticia interrupted:

'You won't believe this,' she said.

Her mother continued:

'This is still difficult for me to talk about; it caused me so much suffering. Well when the baby was born and I went to register her they wanted to put my husband's name on the birth certificate. I told them that they couldn't do that because he was not the father. They said if I wanted my name on the birth certificate I also had to have my husband's name. We argued for a bit then they asked me the father's name. I told them and they wrote his name in as the father and put the mother as unknown. I told them that it was wrong; that I was the mother, but they wouldn't listen. How could they put "mother unknown", when I was standing there right in front of them?'

Remembering those days was obviously painful and she broke off to wipe her eyes and drink some more of the herbal tea.

'You know how in Spain every child has two surnames, the first is the father's name and the second the mother's. Well she had both surnames from her father,' Leticia explained.

'Then when she was four years old something even worse happened; her father came and took her away. He had married by then and he and his wife wanted her to live with them. I could do nothing. I had no rights whatsoever over my child; my name did not appear on any document as her mother. It broke my heart when they took her away.'

'What about now?' I asked. 'Do you see her now?'

'Oh yes. When she became twenty-one she changed her name to include my name in her surname. She is a lovely girl. She lives in the Canary Islands and works as an air-traffic controller, but she keeps in touch with me and her sisters.'

'She had an unhappy childhood,' added Leticia. 'Her stepmother was an alcoholic; she had three children and treated my sister a bit like Cinderella.'

'What about your husband? Did he help you financially?' I asked Jeanette.

'No, he gave us nothing. It was hard bringing up three children on my own; neither their father nor his family would give us any economic support and so I had to work. I was a language teacher and I ran three language schools, two in Málaga and one in Torremolinos. They were part of the Berlitz Language School and were very successful; I employed twenty-seven people at one point, but in the end it all became too difficult employing so many people, what with the taxes etc. So I gave it all up and moved to New York for three years, taking my daughters with me. I wanted to study for my doctorate in languages.

Well in 1986 my husband decided he would like a divorce. By then he had met an Englishwoman and he wanted to marry her. I didn't care; I just let him divorce me. But you know I still don't know if my divorce papers were ever finalised,' she added. 'We were married in Paris, so the papers should be there. Not that it matters now; I won't be getting married again at my age.'

'Oh we'll find a boyfriend for you *Abuela*. A nice one that smokes a lot and loves the bull fight,' her granddaughter said, laughing in the knowledge that these were her grandmother's greatest antipathies.

At this point Jeannette said it was time for her to go home; she lived in a flat in Torremolinos and wanted to avoid the Sunday evening rush hour traffic. Before we said our goodbyes Leticia turned to her daughter:

'Do you have anything to say to Joan about what life is like for women in Spain nowadays?' she asked her daughter with a smile.

Mer smiled back and looked thoughtful:

'Well,' the eight-year old said. 'The boys are always saying that we aren't as strong as them and that we're no good at sports and we can't run as fast.'

'I don't think things have changed very much,' I said. 'I remember the boys in my class saying much the same thing.'

A few minutes later Leticia and I set off for the park.

'It will be cooler in the park and much quieter,' she explained, adding that although I had not met them, she had three other children in the flat who until then had been unusually quiet.

We settled ourselves on a park bench and began to talk. Leticia explained that she had had a rather unconventional childhood; she had found herself living in two different worlds.

'I don't think I'm your typical Spanish woman. My mother was French and a hippy; she was a very liberal and open person, who had travelled a lot and had lots of foreign friends. My father and his family on the other hand were Spanish, very conservative and traditional in their ways; they criticised my mother continually. I'm sure they thought she was a bit mad. I have to admit I sometimes found it rather difficult.

I think I have grown up with both viewpoints. I am like my mother in lots of ways but I am also quite conservative and classical in others. I suppose I was lucky because I was brought up in a very open way at a time when the rest of Spain was quite closed. It was not usual in Franco's time to have such open access to Europe and the world, but Torremolinos was different from the rest of Spain; it had a very international atmosphere and I was able to enjoy the free spirit of the times. I had lots of friends who had Spanish fathers and foreign mothers, so I had access to different attitudes and ideas. I also saw a lot of my father because his shop was in Torremolinos, not far from where we lived. I had to pass it on my way home from school, so I would call in and see him each day.

The first school I went to was when I was six years old. All the girls were taught in one room and the boys in another; at playtime we all met in the playground together. I remember one playtime I went up to the nun that was on duty to tell her that my mother had a baby in her tummy. Those were my exact words. The nun looked at me, horrified and I was immediately taken off to be punished. I had to kneel and hold out my arms in the shape of the cross for what seemed like hours. There was no sex education in my day; we were taught that the stork brought babies from Paris, not that they came out of our mother's tummy. When my mother arrived to take me home she was furious to see me kneeling like that and removed me from the school that very day.

Almost all the schools were private in those days because there were not many public schools and they were only for the very poor. Most schools were single sex schools, run by nuns or priests and were very strict, but my next school was more open and liberal; it was the Rudolph Steiner School and specialised in music and art. From the age of nine I began to play the piano then the guitar and I did courses in flamenco and dance. Some were private classes and some within the school. I had always been exposed to good music; there was always lots of music at home, especially classical music and my mother liked to sing. She belonged to a choir, but never sang professionally.

When I became too old for the Rudolph Steiner School my mother sent me to another convent school; it was alright, the nuns were nice but everything was a lot greyer there than in my old school. Everything seemed a bit sadder and dull. By the time I moved to college Franco had died and of course everything began to change. That was about the time my mother decided to move to New York. I was seventeen so I attended a local High School in New York for a year before taking a place at the University of Indiana. I did a year and a half at university then returned to Madrid to finish my degree in Classical Guitar. When I graduated I began work as a teacher. I worked in Madrid for about ten years until I had a family of my own.

I met my husband when we were both attending a course on personal development; I remember he was in the swimming pool when I first saw him. I never really wanted to combine motherhood and working; I wanted to experience the complete enjoyment of motherhood. So when our first child, Gabriel, was born, I gave up my job and we moved out of Madrid, into a small village in the mountains. We lived a very simple life, selling natural products like honey and chickpeas; my husband also worked with ecological fruit and I continued to have children. I had four children in four years, all by natural means. Gabriel was born in hospital in Madrid; I suppose that was because he was the first and I didn't know what to expect, but he was born so quickly that I thought this is easy. So when I became pregnant again I decided to have the baby at home with my husband to help me. After all I wasn't ill, I was only giving birth. In the end I had all the others at home too. I believe in giving my children as natural a start in life as I can. My family criticise me for not having them vaccinated, but I think they are fine as they are; they are all very healthy children.

We were very happy living in the country; we had little money but a good life. Then when the youngest was four years old we decided we ought to move because my husband needed work. We moved to the Sierra de Ronda, not far from Málaga and he got a job in a hotel. I still wanted us to live in the country, but as the children got older I decided it was better for us to be in the town and that's why we rented this flat in Velez; it's very convenient for their schools and friends.

I've not had a fixed job since Gabriel was born but I give lots of concerts and play at weddings and parties. It's a good time right now because the government is doing a lot for women at the moment. I'm hoping to take advantage of a government scheme that is helping women start up their own businesses. Because I compose my own music I want to form a group with my friend Lucho and my brother-in-law. If I formalise it as a company I can receive grants for setting it up and for publicity.'

I remembered Lucho from the party. He is from Ecuador and plays a number of South American instruments; sometimes he joins Leticia in a duet. I had never met her brother-in-law.

'The government also pays me a family allowance because I have what they term a "*familia numerosa*", more than three children. It's not a lot though, only an eighth of what I would receive anywhere else in Europe. I think it comes to..'

She paused, counting up in her head:

'Twenty-four euros a month for each child, but they pay me every six months so it feels like more. I could go back to working full time but I prefer to spend more time with the children even if it does mean we live close to the breadline.'

I thought of the rather Spartan flat where we had just had tea.

'What about your husband?' I asked.

'We're separated,' she replied. 'We split up about a year ago. At the moment we are waiting for the divorce to go through, but it seems to be taking a long time. We're still good friends; it was just a decision we had to take so that we could both grow more. We were holding each other back.

I suppose it took him a long time to really realise what having children meant. When I first met him one of the things I liked about him was that he was independent; he could cook, wash and iron his own clothes, but when we got married he somehow forgot how to do any of it. I thought of him as an open, modern person, but now I see him as more "*macho*". My sister has children and her husband is wonderful with them; he does everything for them and seems to enjoy it. But I think he is unusual for a Spanish man. I am trying to train my own son to clean and wash up. He will do it if I tell him, but my daughters just do it naturally, without being told.

The last few years had become very tense at home. I think it is better for the children that this tension has gone but I can see that they miss their father. He has moved to Barcelona but he telephones them and sends them emails and every so often he comes to see them.

I suppose I had begun to spend more and more time on my music and he couldn't understand it. "Why do you have to spend so much time on your music?" he would ask again and again. He didn't understand.

Another issue was that he likes to live in the country; he is very religious and likes to live close to nature. I like that too but for my music I have to live near people; it's important for me to live in the town. I know our flat is not very special but it is so convenient for the children and for me.'

She sighed and smiled sadly at me:

'I suppose it's a bit like a repeat of my mother's story: no husband and having to bring up four children. I'm happy but sometimes life is difficult. When you've been married you miss the warmth of a relationship and having someone by your side to turn to. But that doesn't mean I'm about to look for someone on the Internet. I suppose I'm a bit romantic; I would like to meet someone and fall in love, but it's got to be reciprocal. I'm not interested in getting married again just for the sake of getting married. Love is more important to me. I suppose I'm a bit idealistic in that respect. What I would like is to fall in love and watch my creativity shoot up. Yes that's it: fall in love and write six poems.'

She laughed and stood up. The interview was over.

Permiso Marital

Franco's government, which ruled from 1939 to his death in 1975 was that of a dictatorship; all democratic ideas were repressed and the domination of women was part of this trend. Both the government and the Catholic Church wanted to return women to their place as homemakers and mothers and to preserve a conservative and patriarchal structure of the family. They promoted the idea of the woman as "perfecta casada" (the perfect married woman) and "angel de hogar", (the angel of the home) to emphasis and reinforce this idea in society at large and women were expected to enrol in a six-month training course to prepare them for the important role of motherhood. Working women were heavily discriminated against and their career opportunities considerably restricted. A set of laws, known as "permiso marital" (marital permission) were introduced which prohibited married women from working, owning property and travelling without the permission of their husbands. They could not start a business, enter into any type of contract or open a bank account. Even if they had brought their own money into the marriage they were no longer able to dispose of it without their husbands' permission, nor did they have any control over their joint possessions. Worse still, the mother did not share what was called "patria potestad", paternal authority over her own children, only the father had that. If she left the family home, even for a few days, without her husband's permission it was tantamount to desertion and he could call the police to bring her back. Women who committed adultery could receive a penalty of between six months and six years in prison, but the law was considerably more lenient with erring husbands. They were only punished if they made their adultery flagrantly obvious; if they were discreet nothing was said. Abortion was also a crime and divorce impossible. All marriages had to take place in the Catholic Church and as the Church did not recognise divorce the only way anyone could escape from a marriage was through annulment. A wife trapped in an unhappy marriage had no way out.

ARAZELE, MARI JESUS, MARGO, PAOLA, MARIBEL and PILAR.

One day Paola suggested I go to her house to meet some of her friends and drink some tea. They were all women in their fifties and apart from Margo, who was married, lived alone. We sat around a table in the lounge with the French windows pulled right back to let the smoke that was already turning the air blue, drift outside; only two of us were non-smokers. Paola had a two month old West Highland puppy and before anything else could begin we all had to examine and comment on this new addition to the household. This was followed by everyone in turn pulling out their mobile phones to show photographs of their own pampered pooches. The preliminaries dispensed with and cups of tea or glasses of beer handed around, we began.

Arazele, or Ara as she liked to be called, was the first to speak. She was a plump, homely looking woman with sparkling eyes and dimples in her cheeks. She had been married for twenty years before her husband decided he wanted a younger woman and had left her for his secretary.

'My own parents were happily married, but even if they hadn't been they couldn't have divorced or separated anyway. It just didn't happen then. When you got married you remained married until one of you died.'

'Well my parents never spoke of having a happy marriage; we never spoke of such intimate things in our family. I think they were happy because it sounds as if they were in love when they married. I remember my mother said that they met in *Calle Larios*, walking along one day, all the girls together and the boys with their mates, parading up and down like they used to in those days and my mother started up a conversation with him using her fan,' joined in Pilar.

She rotated her wrist as if fanning herself.

'You know there is a complete sign language of the fan; in those days women knew how to communicate all sorts of messages through the different movements of the fan. Well that is how my parents began to speak to each other.'

Maribel, the only one present who had never been married added:

'My mother got married because she had reached an age when she thought she would have to marry or remain single all her life; she was thirty. That was very old then; you were in danger of becoming an old maid. She wasn't in love with my father and she was older than him.'

She laughed.

'It's funny because she has always lied about her age. During the Civil War lots of documents got lost and so she took advantage of that to take a few years off. We didn't find out her true age until she had died and my sister went to sort out the inheritance.'

'I don't think my parents were in love at first,' continued Ara. 'My mother married to leave home. My grandfather was a tyrant; he wouldn't let my mother or her sisters leave the house, they weren't allowed to use make-up or go out with their friends. He kept them completely locked up. But despite that my mother managed to get out without him knowing and she met my father. My father was a good man, so after three months she said to him: "Either we get married or I'll have to stop seeing you because of my father."'

'Yes but lots of fathers behaved like that because they wanted to protect their daughters; it's the same today,' Pilar commented.

This started a lively discussion about their own daughters and the need for them to be given more protection than their sons.

'Yes but is it being protective or being *machista*?' asked Ara.

'A bit of both, I think,' replied Margo. 'Even today lots of women go to work and still have to do everything in the home; the majority of men do nothing to help.'

'Well I don't agree with that. I taught my son how to look after himself; he can even sew. I'm not very good at sewing but I taught him how to sew on a button and fix a hem, simple things.'

'I think the boys today are more *machista* than ever,' said Ara.

'I don't agree. My son even phones me to ask for recipes so that he can prepare the evening meal. He and his girlfriend work together in the same company and if she has to work late he cooks the meal. He'll ring me up and say: "How do you make *pollo al ajillo* or *tortilla patata?*" He wants to learn.'

'Yes but he's older. Boys today, adolescents, they are tremendously machista.'

'My son isn't,' insisted Pilar. 'My father was more *machista* than him. If my brothers did not study there was hell to play but if I didn't study it didn't matter. My father would just smile and say: "Don't worry; it doesn't matter you'll be getting married one day anyway." If he had told me to study I would have and I'd have been able to get a better job.'

'I'm not sure there's equality in the job market anyway, despite what the socialist government say,' said Margo steering the conversation onto a different tack.

'There's certainly more women in the universities than men,' Ara added.

'Yes but the economy is still dominated by men,' said Mari Jesus, who works as a civil servant in the Department of Culture.

'Particularly in estate agencies, women are the first to get the sack when sales are slack; it's a totally male world,' agreed Pilar, who worked for a small estate agency.

'My niece applied for a job as an engineer; she was very well qualified, having taken second place in the national exams. She had to go before a tribunal made up entirely of men, old men. It was the first time a woman had put herself forward for this particular job. Of course she failed; they turned her down despite her excellent qualifications. It's a very closed environment. Then at an interview for another job she was asked if she was planning to have any children.'

Mari Jesus was obviously angry at the injustice her niece had suffered.

'I don't think they're allowed to ask you that,' interrupted Ara.

'Look I'm a woman and I can sympathise with working women but the problem arises when an employee becomes pregnant. I know it sounds *machista* but it can be very difficult for a small firm; it can cost them a lot. Zapatero has done well appointing a pregnant woman as a minister but it is different for large companies and organisations, they have other employees that can cover and do the work; for small companies it can be disastrous,' argued Margo.

'But the companies get help from the government.'

'Yes but women are allowed more time off now, three months.'

'I've got this problem right now,' said Paola, who had just sat down again after replenishing everyone's drinks. 'My marketing assistant is due to have her baby in September. On Monday she told me that the doctor had signed her off work because she has sciatica, caused by the pregnancy. So now she is going to be off work until September, then another three months that she is entitled to after that; she won't be back until the New Year at the earliest. The problem is not the money; it's what do I do in the meantime. The marketing for the school has to be done between September and April to be of any use, so she will not be really effective until September of 2009. I'm obliged to keep her job for her until she returns, although I wouldn't want to get rid of her anyway just because she was having a baby, but it is not easy to find anyone to do the work on a temporary basis. So that means we do no marketing this year. Like Margo says, if you are a big company you can manage with someone being off such a long time, but for me it's going to be very difficult.

I can understand her situation because I'm a woman but women today have many more rights than in my day. I worked and when I was pregnant I had two months off, but we didn't have such comprehensive cover as nowadays. In my opinion there's a great difference between our generation and the women of today.

For example, how do I know how much pain she is suffering with her sciatica. The Social Security is very quick to sign people off work.'

'Yes, but it's the same for a man.'

'Statistically,' began Mari Jesus. 'There is a statistic that says that many more men than women fail to go to work on Monday mornings, because they have had a heavy weekend.

I heard it on the radio; they said that women are better workers than men.'

Paola was still thinking about her own problem:

'I couldn't sack a pregnant woman. I am a woman and I've had to struggle to get where I am; so I understand.'

'Do you know that Spain is one of the countries with the lowest birth rate?' Ava volunteered.

'Well there are lots of immigrants,' said Pilar.

I asked them what they thought about there being so many cases of domestic violence in the news.

'Well there's always been domestic violence,' said Ara. 'In the old days you couldn't get a separation so women had to put up with it. Now they are standing up for themselves and saying "No more", but as soon as they try to get a separation the husband kills them.'

'Do you know that up until now not a single case of domestic psychological abuse has been won in Spain. There have been lots of cases but they have been difficult to prove. Married women are unable to do anything about it,' Pilar added.

'If we are truthful we could all say that we have been psychologically maltreated.'

'But it's much worse than physical abuse because you can't see the damage. When I lived in the Canaries my husband abused me psychologically and I couldn't do anything about it. I had to give all my money to him and he spent it on gambling and other women, but he wasn't seen as an abusive husband.'

'Yes Pilar, but where there's no proof there's no case,' replied Mari Jesus.

'Because there's never been a judge who would rule on it. You need to suffer the abuse for twenty years before you have a chance of proving it and by then you're screwed. And anyway all the psychologists are men.'

'A husband was always regarded as a good husband as long as he didn't hit you and didn't get drunk. Your parents would say he was a good man.'

'If he had money, you ate well and he didn't hit you, you were considered to be fine.'

'Years ago women had no economic independence so they were weak; they had no rights. I think domestic abuse has always been there, absolutely. This is a *macho* society where the man has the economic power, he has the force and he makes the decisions. If you think that domestic violence has increased it is only because it was hidden before. Marital problems were usually sorted out within the family. Women had no money, couldn't leave, were looked down on by society and they married for life, be it good or bad. Men never thought that an abused woman would stand up for herself,' explained Mari Jesus.

'Yes and when she does, he kills her,' repeated Ara.

At this point Paola brought in some food: plates of cheese and ham, olives and nuts. The discussion was put on hold while we changed from tea to wine and had our glasses generously filled.

Mari Jesus resumed the conversation; she was in a hurry to leave as she had to go to work. Her department had organised a series of poetry evenings at a theatre in Málaga and she had to arrive before ten o'clock.

'Many women of our generation are divorced or separated and now they want their own life, especially once their children have left home. I was married for twenty-four years and I've been divorced for four. When I was a teenager I went to university and took my degree, but there were few opportunities for work, so I got married and became a housewife. I had three children in quick succession and spent my life looking after them. My husband was a very conservative man, very protective and completely *machista*. He controlled me completely and would not allow me to develop at all, in any way. His treatment towards me could certainly be described as psychological abuse but I could do nothing about it.

Then when my children had grown up I started work and as soon as I had some economic stability I decided to divorce him. My father would not have approved, but he's dead and my mother is not really aware of what's happened. My sister is very religious and doesn't believe in divorce but she still backed me; I've always had the backing of my family.

Am I happy? Yes, I'm happy with what I've done, but truly happy? I don't know. At least now I make the decisions; first it was my father making decisions for me, then my boyfriend, then my husband; now I make the decisions.'

She laughed.

'Well, my mother as well, my boss and my children, but mostly me.'

I asked them why they thought so many young people didn't want to get married these days.

'They've never lived religion; they never felt the control of the Church,' replied Mari Jesus. 'They have never lived in a totally protective state and don't experience the same level of all-encompassing protection from their parents.'

The conversation moved briefly to religion and the Church.

'No, my family is not religious, except for my mother who was very Christian and a sister who was very deep into the

Church. Neither my father nor my brother went to Mass,' offered Maribel.

'It was mostly women who went to church; the men didn't go.'

'No that's true, but it was a world of men; the Catholic Church has always kept women down.'

'Religion has always done a lot of harm.'

'Not so much religion, as the Church.'

'You know even very traditional parents accept their daughters living together these days, not just in the cities, but in the villages too,' said Paola, bringing the conversation back to marriage.

'My daughter practically lives with her boyfriend but she says she wants to get married eventually.'

Ara had two daughters, non-identical twins, age thirty-one. The one she had been referring to was a ballerina and taught classical dance at a school in Seville. The boyfriend worked in Málaga, so their relationship was curtailed to weekends only. The other daughter was a doctor of philosophy and was currently doing research on women, equality and multi-cultures. She had been awarded a grant to study in Finland and was there until the end of the year when she was due to take up a post as a teacher at the University of Málaga.

'She's having an argument with the university because they want to put her title as Dr. and she says it should be Dra. She doesn't have a boyfriend. Well I say that but in fact one week before she left for Finland she met this boy at a conference and they have been writing emails and telephoning ever since. So maybe.'

'My daughter says she will never get married,' interrupted Margo.

'Well my mother never said I had to get married,' commented Ara.

'Mine neither.'

'My mother wanted me to get married so that she wouldn't have to worry about me anymore; she wanted my husband to worry about me instead,' said Maribel.

'My mother was very open-minded in that respect. I don't know if it was because of her own experience, but I do know she talked more about a boyfriend she had had during the war than she did about my father,' continued Ara.

'When I was thirty and still a spinster, my mother told me that if I ever decided to get married I should remember two things: that I had always had my own way and that nobody had ever told me what to do,' said Maribel.

'Yes but that was your mother. But haven't you felt as far as society is concerned that you're a strange bird, still unmarried at your age? A spinster. Don't tell me you haven't felt this,' said Paola with some feeling.

'It's never affected me.'

Maribel had her own business, a fashion shop. She had had lovers and boyfriends over the years; in 1988 she had met Bruno, an Italian who had come to Málaga to learn Spanish and she had had a love affair with him for sixteen years, visiting him in Milan or seeing him in Málaga. She had never wanted to get married.

'But women of our age that have never been married and have no children, people regard them as strange,' Paola insisted.

'Some frustration maybe.'

'Nowadays it's different. In my mother's days there weren't any spinsters; they were all old maids. And besides which it was always considered the woman's fault, that she had not been able to catch a man.'

'Yes and from quite a young age, at twenty-five you were considered an old maid,' added Ara.

'It's like in Morocco; there if a girl reaches twenty-five and she's not married it's a sacrilege because she's born to marry and have children. I've a sister who's single and she's regarded as a bit strange. Nowadays it's different; women want to remain single.'

'You only have to look at the apartments they are building these days; they're not family houses, they're small, suitable for two or three people.'

'You know my husband wanted us to remain living in the same house after we had divorced. He suggested that he should live on the ground floor and I live upstairs. He said it made sense economically.'

'And did you?'

'Not likely. We divorced and went our separate ways. Later I did meet someone else and we went out together for six years, but we never lived together.'

'What happened to him?'

'Well it wasn't going anywhere; he was in his sixties and separated, but he had a nine year old child from his second marriage. It was chaotic trying to organise my life around that. I had dedicated most of my life to my own children, now I wanted to have some time for my own life, for my painting.'

'Well it's impossible to meet anyone in Málaga and form a relationship,' complained Pilar.

Pilar was the daughter of a military officer and had been born in Málaga; she had a strict upbringing and had married a doctor in order to get away from home.

'I left Málaga to go to the Canaries with my husband and now I'm back. I'm divorced; my kids are in Madrid; my friends are all married. What is there for me? I was only twenty-two when I married. Twenty-five years I devoted to my family and now what? Even the flat I had in Málaga was occupied by a sitting tenant and it's taken me five years to get him out. I tell you those five years were awful; I had to spend most of my time outdoors. I couldn't spend all my time in those dreadful rooms so I was out all day and every evening. I'm too old for that. I was exhausted. At least now I have my own place.'

'The trouble is that the men you can meet in bars are only interested in one-night stands; they want sex not a relationship.'

'They go out to enjoy themselves and they are looking for younger women.'

'Yes, even the sixty-year olds stand at the bar, with a drink in one hand and a fag in the other, eyeing up the young girls.'

'Well I don't like to go to bars at night anymore. If I just wanted sex I could pay for it. Ring a ..'

'A gigolo,' someone suggested.

'Yes, ring a gigolo and get myself a real man instead of an old guy.'

'I'd just like some affection,' Ara said wistfully, as she finished her glass of wine.

Divorce

The Second Republic had made divorce legal stating in its guidelines of 1931 that "marriage is based upon equality of rights of both sexes and can be dissolved by mutual consent or upon the petition of any of both spouses."

However when Franco came to power the Second Republic's reforms were reversed. In 1938 he repealed the act introduced by the Second Republic six years previously where divorce could be obtained by mutual agreement and he invalidated all divorce decrees that had been awarded during that time; he suspended any pending divorce or separation petitions, removed the right of women to have a different nationality from their husbands and annulled all civil marriages. He specified in the new Civil Code that "A man must protect his wife and she must obey her husband."

Breaking up a marriage during Franco's rule became a complicated, lengthy and very expensive process. The only way a couple could be divorced was to get their marriage annulled on the grounds of either impotence, that one of them had been underage at the time of the marriage or that they had been forced into getting married. Even if only one of the partners was a Catholic the marriage would have been sanctioned by the Catholic Church and was subject to the same restrictions as any other. Obtaining a legal separation was the only way out for many Spaniards and even that was not easy as the aim of the court officials and even the judge was to reunite the couple, not separate them; it could take anything from two to eight years to obtain the separation. This too was often out of the economic reach of most working people. As a church guide of the period put it: "to love is to endure", a new wife was advised to avoid confrontation and to give way to her husband at all times.

In 1978 the new democratic government established laws to regulate everything to do with marriage: the age of the participants, their capacity to contract it, duties and rights of the spouses, causes of separation and the division of communal goods. Although a survey done in 1975 showed that 71% of Spaniards wanted divorce to be made easier it was not until 1981 that it was legalised. The civil code was modified to allow the rupture of a marriage in three forms, through annulment as before, through a legal separation and through divorce. There were two routes that could be taken for a divorce to take place: in the first the couple had to have been living apart for two years by mutual agreement or for five years if only one partner agreed; the second was by applying directly for a legal separation on the grounds of cruelty, adultery or desertion. One year after they had obtained a legal separation the couple were free to apply for a divorce, providing that one of them was culpable. This notion of culpability often meant hiring private detectives to catch the guilty party in the act, or even staging the scene with mutual agreement. Unfortunately the law contained no provision to punish defaulters in the payment of alimony.

Once the new act became law there were thousands of petitions for divorce, more than half from women. Despite this however, between 1981 and 1994 Spain continued to have one of the lowest divorce rates in Europe. This was because many Spaniards still preferred to have a legal separation, partly because of the costs involved but also because of the social stigma that still clung to divorced women; they preferred separation or the "Spanish divorce", as it became known.

In 2005 the divorce law was modified again, placing more emphasis on the will of individuals to divorce and removing the need for a guilty party. Petitioners could opt for separation if they chose but were able to go straight to the divorce stage after only being married three months; it became known as the "express divorce" bill. One of the arguments for making the whole process easier was that almost half of the domestic violence that occurred was in homes where the couple were going through the long process of separation. A survey taken by the National Institute of Statistics the following year indicated that the number of divorces had risen by 74.3% since the new law had come into force.

BLANCA PALOMA born in Ceuta in 1960

Paloma was born in Ceuta but moved to mainland Spain when she was quite young. She lived in Barcelona for many years and now lives in Málaga. She is 48 years old, married and has two grown-up sons. She works as a yoga teacher.

It was a bright spring morning when my new neighbour, Paloma, as she liked to be called, came round to see me. She had been delighted at my request to tell me something about her life and was eager to get started. I set up my voice recorder on the terrace table, hoping I had positioned it close enough to pick up her soft, gentle voice and that the swallows intent on nesting under the eaves of my terrace roof would not drown us out with their constant singing. We were sitting in the sun but I calculated that it would be at least an hour before it became so hot we would have to move.

Paloma was my yoga teacher and she sat in the wicker chair, with her back straight and one leg folded under her, looking relaxed and serene. She was one of the calmest people I knew and it surprised me to hear her say, with a touch of agitation in her voice that she had many things to tell me about her childhood, some good and some bad.

'Well as you already know I was actually born in Ceuta, in North Africa, but I left there when I was only one year old, so I don't consider myself a *Ceutana*,' she began. 'All I know about our time there was what I've been told. We were a big family; there were lots of aunts and uncles, cousins, my grandmother and my parents all living together. In the early sixties there was no work in Ceuta so one of my uncles went to Barcelona to look for a job; he wrote back and told us that we would all be better off in Barcelona where there was plenty of work, so the whole family decided to move there.

We moved to a village on the outskirts of the city called Sant Boi and found a house in an area favoured by immigrants; there were people there from all over Spain, particularly from Badajoz. My grandmother moved in with my parents, myself and my three brothers and the rest of the family found houses nearby.

In Ceuta my grandmother had been a seamstress; she had made high class clothing and had a number of girls working for her, sewing the clothes. Ceuta was a military base and all the officers' wives would come to her to have their dresses made. When the day was over and the sewing girls had gone home she would hold spiritualist meetings in her salon and invite mediums and like-minded friends to attend. Her own family didn't believe in spiritualism, so she tried to keep these meetings secret. My father thought it was ridiculous and my aunt was an atheist; she was very anti-Catholic and hated anything to do with the church, which she considered to be very false. I think this was partly to do with the stories she had heard about the nuns and priests in Ceuta having sex and murdering any babies that were born. I never knew if it was true or not but I hated it when she told me that; I tried to put it out of my mind.

Anyway all her life, my grandmother had been interested in different types of religions and was continually looking into some aspect or other. By the time we moved to Spain she had quarrelled with the Catholic Church and had instead become very interested in the Jehovah's Witnesses; she loved it when they came to visit her. I can remember her sitting at the living room table with one of these well dressed young men in their dark suits, sitting on each side of her and the Bible on the table between them. She loved to discuss things in the Bible that puzzled her and I'm sure they learnt as much from her as she did from them.

My grandmother was a very strong-minded woman but although she ruled the rest of the family, she spoiled my father, who was her only son. Surrounded by sisters he was very much a "mother's boy". My grandmother was also a very frugal woman and when she lived in Ceuta she saved her money and food so that she would always have some to give to people when they needed it; she was very generous to those in need. People would often say "Let's go and see if Luciana has any sugar or some flour." They knew she would never turn them away. There was a Moor who came to the house selling eggs, a poor woman with many children, and my grandmother would often give her something to eat.

My grandmother lived with us until she died; I was about twelve then. I don't remember her dying because when she became ill we children were sent to stay with an aunt until it was over. But I do remember her room was filled with all the personal things she had brought from Ceuta, such as an enormous collection of buttons, threads and multi coloured materials, some with giant floral designs on them. As a child I found them fascinating. She would sometimes ask me to clean her room for her because she had trouble moving about. When she was a child a horse had kicked her in the back and she had been left with a permanently deformed spine as the result of the accident. She loved to listen to the radio, especially the news and although she was very anti-Franco she always insisted on listening to what he had to say.

Well when my parents arrived in Barcelona my father found work as a builder and my mother began to work from home, sewing tailored trousers. My grandmother helped my mother run the house because there was too much for my mother to do on her own, looking after four children and sewing until late at night.

Women attending a Singer sewing machine course

My mother was always the strong one in our family; my father was more easy-going. They had met in Ceuta when my mother came over on holiday from Málaga to visit her aunt. They fell in love and she stayed in Ceuta and married him. I think she found Barcelona a big change from Ceuta, which was a fairly quiet town; Barcelona was noisy with lots of tall apartment blocks and a great deal of traffic.

Being brought up with three brothers was not easy; I remember that on Sundays my brothers would go out into the street to meet their friends and play and I would have to stay in the house and clean. Sometimes Papa would see me and smile and then he'd bend down and give me a kiss and say "Not much more to do," but he never let me go out until I had finished. I don't think my mother was very happy; she worked very hard, her family were all a long way away in Málaga and she didn't get on with my father. He wasn't abusive or a drunk, but he liked to go to the bar and meet his friends and have a few drinks. On a Sunday he would not get home until after three and by then we would have eaten, so he would eat alone and he would behave a bit like a spoilt child if his food was not exactly as he liked it.

Then when I was about eight or nine my mother decided to take us to Málaga for a summer holiday. We went by train. My mother's sister was very pleased to see us and gave us two rooms in her big house to stay in; she said we could come and visit her every summer. It was wonderful; we all loved it, especially my father. Her house was very close to the beach and all along the promenade there were little beach bars, *chiringitos*; my father would sit in the bar with a glass of

wine, chatting to his friends and looking at his family, his children playing in the sea and his wife sunbathing on the beach. He was very pleased to have all his family around him and not have to do anything himself. It was a rest for my mother and she was always happier when she was there.

Mama always worked so hard but she had a very good head for business. One day she decided to stop sewing trousers at home and bought herself a shop space in a big market; it was actually like an enormous warehouse with a butcher's stall, a frozen fish shop, a baker's shop, a greengrocers and lots of other shops. It was a sort of co-operative. Mama opened a shop selling haberdashery, wool and lengths of material. Of course the shop was not busy all the time, so when it was quiet she knitted jumpers and cardigans then sold them to her customers. It became very successful and women would come in and order exactly what they fancied having made. They would say things like: "I'd like something with a flower here," or "Maybe some stripes would be nice"; all the garments were made to measure and when they were finished Mama would press them ready for the women to try on. They usually came round to our house on a Sunday afternoon to try them and if they didn't fit Mama would make the adjustments for the next Sunday. Her customers were all local women and so she had a lot of repeat orders. They weren't rich women, just ordinary working-class people, who wanted something special now and again. Much of what Mama made was hand knitted but she also made things with a knitting machine and sold them at a cheaper price.

It's funny but my mother never wanted me to be a seamstress. She never had time to show me how to sew or how to knit. Once when I was about fourteen I saw a picture of this black and white jumper that I really liked. I asked her to show me how to knit it, but she wouldn't. "I'm far too busy," she said each time I asked. This upset me because she always had time to teach her customers how to knit; they would come into her shop to buy wool and confess that they didn't know what to do with it, so she would show them. I used to sit in the shop watching how she did it, watching and watching until I knew the moves. But I wanted that jumper so much that in the end I stole some wool and needles from the shop and went to my aunt's house and asked her to help me. She was a bit surprised but she helped me to get started. Unfortunately when it came to finishing off the neck neither my aunt nor I knew how to do it, so I had to go to Mama and ask her. I was really nervous; I said:

"Mama can you help me with something?"

"What?" she said, without looking at me.

I pulled the jumper out of my bag and said: "This.".

She was astonished when she saw the jumper.

"Did you make that?" she asked.

I nodded.

"Where did you get the wool?"

Then I had to confess, but she was so amazed that I had knitted the jumper that she was not cross with me at all.'

Paloma stopped and stood up to move her chair out of the sun; she looked a little sad.

'There's something I'd like to tell you now but it's not very pleasant,' she said. 'I suppose that my mother was not a happy woman, she had to work very hard and my father did not give her a lot of support; it was always her who had to punish us, not my father. She would often hit us, but he never did; he just laughed and joked with us. I suppose he was a bit irresponsible.

Well when I was eleven or twelve, it was a time when I would have liked to have been able to talk to my mother about things that were worrying me and I felt a great need for some affection from her, but she was always too busy for me. That's when I first started going to visit my aunt Aurora; she too was busy, always at home sewing for her family but she had plenty of time to talk to me. I was happy in her house and we spent a lot of time together, chatting about all sorts of things. I loved to talk to her and because I couldn't talk to my mother I confided in her.

Then one day I met this boy; he was twenty and I was twelve. We liked each other very much and used to talk all the time. I suppose he became a bit fixated on me; although I was only twelve I had a lot more body than I have now.'

She moved her hands along her slim figure to show me how much curvier she had been before she took up yoga.

'But there was no romance; I just liked to talk to him. He was always so kind and he never tried to take advantage of me. Well one day my mother found out that I'd been talking to him and she lost her temper and made me stay in the house. However she couldn't watch me all the time and I continued to see this boy. Then one day she was angry about something and hit me and I just decided I couldn't stand it anymore; I left home and went to stay with the boy. I was only twelve.'

She looked at me in horror at what she had done.

'I ran to him crying and saying that my parents beat me and that I needed his help. He was very kind; he took me to his sister's house and we stayed with her and her family for a week. Then one day we were in a neighbouring village and as I passed the bus stop I saw my aunt Aurora's husband get off the bus. I grabbed the boy's hand and screamed "Run, run"; I made him run away as fast as we could, but my uncle came after us and caught me. I was hysterical and the boy couldn't understand why I was like that, but it was because I was terrified of my uncle.

Some years before, when I was only eight, he had come into my bedroom. I was off school because I was sick and I was sitting in my bunk bed. My brothers were not there; I was alone. My uncle stood by my bed and slipped his hand under the covers and begun touching me. I froze; I didn't know what to do. Then when he stopped he said:

"Don't ever tell anyone."

I never said anything to anyone; I was too scared. Many years later I heard that he had molested his young sister-in-law as well; I think he may have had a mental problem.'

She paused then added:

'I never spoke about it to anyone; I suppose I felt ashamed. I never even told my husband, Juan, until about four years ago because it hurt so much to think about it.'

She took a drink of water and then continued:

'I suppose this may have influenced my decision to run away; at the time I don't think I felt protected in my own home.

Anyway when my uncle took me home my mother was furious with me, but even more so with the boy. She said it was all his fault. I heard her tell my father that it must have been because I looked so grown-up and lovely; that I looked more of a woman than I actually was. So she decided to send me to a boarding school. I remember crying and crying but she wouldn't change her mind. But first of all she took me to the doctor to see that I was alright; then when she found out that the boy hadn't touched me she relaxed a bit.

In actual fact I really enjoyed going to the boarding school; the children were mostly boys and girls whose parents were separated or working abroad. At weekends we were allowed to go home to our families or they could come and visit us. I spent a happy two years there until my mother decided that the danger had passed and I could return home and go back to a local school. I was sad to leave the school and my friends and especially because my new school was an all-girls' convent school, where the nuns were very strict and we had to wear a school uniform.

One day I was coming out of school and I saw the boy again. I hurried on without speaking to him; I didn't want to get involved in all that again, but he followed me and pushed a love letter into my hand. When I got home I showed it to my mother then went to my room and cried. My mother decided it was time to send me to another boarding school, but instead of letting me go back to the original one she sent me to a very strict convent. I cried and pleaded with her but she wouldn't relent; she blamed it on the boy, saying he wouldn't leave me alone.

I arrived at my new school one Sunday afternoon and the next morning when I went to get washed I noticed one of the girls cleaning the bathroom then I saw another girl cleaning the windows. I asked them what they were doing and they told me that they all had to take it in turns to do the cleaning. We were expected to get up at six o'clock and clean the school before lessons began. I was horrified; I was sure my mother didn't know about this, so I asked if I could 'phone her. I was told no, not until the weekend, so I went from room to room until I found an empty one with a telephone in it and I rang my mother. Two days late she came and took me home. I had felt as though I was in a correction facility not a school and I did not think that I deserved that. So then my mother had to find me yet another school. In the end she decided not to send me to any more boarding schools and personally escorted me to and from the local school each day.

I finished school at fourteen with a basic education but my parents wanted me to study more. I said I was happy to continue studying but I wanted to choose something I liked. I was very, very fond of babies and after a bit of thought I said I wanted to study nursery care at a college in Barcelona. My mother instantly refused; she was not going to allow me to travel to Barcelona every day on my own. She said I would have to study nearer to home. I argued with her that it was only a twenty minute bus ride to the college, but she was adamant. I had to take a secretarial course in the village; it was every evening from six until ten at night.

I didn't like the course but I made some friends. We used to go out together to the disco; there was a young people's disco once a week from six o'clock until nine and my mother allowed me to go to it. That was where I met Juan, my husband; he was twenty-one and I was fifteen.

We fell in love and began to go out together. At first when Juan took me home, it was only to the door, he didn't come in. I told my mother about him but she only said "What boy?" then didn't show any more interest. Then one day my father saw him bring me home and invited him to go with him for a drink, and in that way he became accepted as my boyfriend. He took me to his home to meet his mother and his family and I got on well with them; they especially liked me because I could sew and knit and very soon asked me to teach them.

After about eight or nine months we began to have a sexual relationship; I wasn't interested in sex but Juan explained to me that because he was older he had "his needs". I knew nothing about sex except what my friends talked about and most of that I didn't understand; my mother had not told me anything and they never taught us anything about it in school. Even though it was possible to buy contraceptives by then, I had never heard of them, so it was not surprising that I soon became pregnant. Even then I didn't realise what was happening. I remember lying in bed one day complaining of a pain in my stomach and my mother questioning me. Then she asked me when I had had my last period. When I told her it had been a couple of months, she asked me if I thought I was pregnant. I said I didn't know. I remember she threw up her hands in horror and said: "What am I going to tell your father." Sometimes these sorts of things can bring a family closer together, but not in my case. My father was very immature; he never spoke to me at all about it, ever. Straight away my parents went to speak to Juan's parents and together they decided we should get married. I don't think my parents-in-law were too bothered about the fact that we were having a baby; I think my mother-in-law was more worried about the kind of family her son was marrying into. Luckily when all the parents met they got on quite well; Juan's family was of a similar class to mine.

We had a church wedding, not because Juan and I wanted one but because my mother wanted us to marry in church. My aunt offered to make my wedding dress and took me into Barcelona to choose the material. I began to enjoy the arrangements for the wedding but I felt that the adults wanted to get it over with as quickly as possible and were only too glad when it was all finished and we were finally married. I remember on my wedding day there was a power cut in our neighbourhood and my friend had come to help me do my hair but we couldn't dry it. I was due to get married in an hour and my long hair was hanging down my back, soaking wet, so we walked down to the hairdressers to see if they had any electricity, but they didn't have any either. In the end I had to leave it to dry naturally. It didn't really bother me. After the wedding we had a big family meal and one of the cousins cut off Juan's tie for the *Corvata de Novios*. This is a custom where someone goes round the room snipping off bits of the groom's tie and selling them to the guests. The money they pay is a gift to the bride and groom instead of buying them presents. We used that money to pay for our honeymoon; we went first to see my aunt in Málaga, then to Juan's relatives in Alhama de Granada then to Ceuta. We were away for two weeks.

In the meantime my mother decided to buy a bigger flat above her shop so that Juan and I could live there. While I waited for Claudio to be born I ran the house and my mother worked downstairs in the shop. We lived with my mother for three years then we started looking for our own place.

Claudio was born in hospital; he was such a beautiful baby and so quiet and contented. I had an easy birth, partly because I was so young, only sixteen and also because I have a very wide pelvis. I had to stay in the hospital for three days before I could go home and I was very bored. But I loved being home with my baby; he made me so happy. Each day when it was time for a siesta I would lie next to him and just gaze at him; I was so happy then.

Eventually we found a small flat near my mother-in-law's and then of course we had to learn how to manage a home for ourselves. I was better at it than Juan who just had no idea. We lived in that flat for three years but during all that time Juan hardly had any work; sometimes he would work in a bar, but then the hours were so long and the money very poor. He just couldn't find any work as a carpenter, so I suggested we give up the flat and move to Málaga where I was sure there was more work. We stayed there a number of years but things were no better so in the end we went back to Barcelona.

Then I met a man called Jaime who had a wool shop and was looking for someone to run it. I began to work for him from six in the morning until eight at night. It was a long day but Claudio ate at school and my mother-in-law used to pick him up in the evening. I missed my son but I enjoyed the work; we did very well in the shop and soon I had to employ a girl to help me. Jaime's main business was supplying the wholesale trade with hand-knitted sweaters, which were then sold in the main shops in Barcelona. He had a number of women knitting for him and when they brought the knitwear into the shop it was my job to check it was alright before we sent it to the wholesaler. Besides that I would draw out the designs for them to knit. Jaime knew everybody in the trade and his business did very well. It was a similar type of shop to my mother's but my mother never had enough work to offer me a job. Anyway after I had been working for Jaime for a year I thought: "Why am I working for this man? I could do this for myself." I talked to Juan about it but he pointed out that it would not be possible for us to open a shop in Barcelona because the rents were too expensive, so we decided to go to Alhama de Granada, the village where Juan was born, and open a shop there.'

Alhama de Granada is a small town high in the mountains in the province of Granada. Here the summers are very hot and the winters very cold. To get to Alhama the road is narrow and difficult; it winds through gorges and up mountains, but once you get there the land spreads out into a wide, fertile plain. In the days of the Moorish occupation this was the area where all the foodstuffs for the city of Granada were grown.

'We lived in a flat that belonged to Juan's family and rented a small shop close by. I suggested to Juan that I handle the shop and the women knitters and he could do the selling. But Juan's response was his usual "*No sé*", he didn't know. Well at first the shop went well. The women in the area were not used to such a modern shop and there was a lot of interest to begin with, but it was never really a great success and we eventually closed it. We opened a second shop in Granada itself and Juan took to the road selling the knitwear in Málaga, Granada, Motril and all the other towns around. Unfortunately for us this was the time when there were a lot of machine knitted sweaters for sale at much cheaper prices and gradually we found we were selling less and less of the hand-made knitwear. It didn't just affect our sales it was a trend all over Spain. One day my mother telephoned and asked "How's sales?" I told her and she said it was just the same in Barcelona, that many wool shops were closing, but she was going to try to hang on a bit longer, at least until she was sixty-three.

So we knew there was no point going back to Barcelona. Then I had an idea. My mother had a house in Málaga that we all used to go to for a month in the summer; the rest of the year it was let but the tenants never took care of the house and as the years went by it was getting more and more run down. I suggested that Juan and I and the children go and live in the house and we would renovate it for her. She agreed; as long as she could still go there in the summer she was happy to see the house better cared for.

So we moved back to Málaga. We had somewhere to live but we still needed work. In that area, close to the beach, there were lots of foreign students. I went to the *Academia Plus* language school and offered to let some rooms to their students. It was a great success; we had two or three students every month; I would give them breakfast and they would eat their evening meal with us. I enjoyed having them there; I met lots of different people, from many countries. Sometimes if they came across something colloquial that they didn't understand I would explain it to them. All the students said that they found me very easy to understand because I spoke more clearly than the local Malagueños, who don't bother to sound their "s"s and their "t"s.

After a while a number of other language schools opened in the area and *Academia Plus* had fewer students to send me, so I tried some other schools, but they said our house was too difficult for the students to get to. The house was up a steep hill, with no access for cars so they would have to walk; part of the road was really just a long flight of steps, just like you would see in little mountain villages. But it was wonderful when you got there; we had a lovely garden that looked out over the Bay of Málaga and across to Torremolinos. Gradually we found that we had fewer and fewer students to stay, Juan had no work and I began to feel that we were getting nowhere. By then we had completely renovated my mother's house but we still did not have a house of our own, and now we had no work either; so once again we decided to move. I suppose I was also a bit homesick; I wanted to live near my mother again. We packed everything we had into one car: books, children, clothes and went back to my mother's. I remember thinking how few possessions we owned after so many years.

By then my father had died and my mother only had my youngest brother, Ernesto, living with her. I thought she was pleased to see us but one morning, only a few months after we had arrived, my mother told us that she and Ernesto were going to live in the house in Málaga and that we could stay on in Barcelona in her house. I couldn't believe it; I had only just come back to Barcelona to be near her and now she was moving away.

One of my friends was working as a cleaner and I started doing the same. After a few months I suggested to her that we team up and work together. In that way we would always have some back up if one of us, or the children was ill, and we could help each other with the work. It was great; it meant there were two of us if a sofa had to be moved for example and there were plenty of jobs that were easier if there were two of you doing them, such as cleaning blinds. We printed some cards and soon got lots of work.

By now Claudio was working and Juan too had some work; there was just Ivan, my second son, still at school. Life should have been better but I was suffering from a lot of stress and I was always tired. My relationship with Juan was suffering too; he worked, I worked and at the weekends we went to bed and had sex but that was it. We never communicated. I suppose he was suffering from stress too, but I knew that I wanted more from my life. Besides which I felt that Ivan was unhappy, so I took him to a psychologist. We both found it very helpful to talk to the psychologist.

That was when I started reading some books on yoga. I asked myself "Does this peace really exist?" I started practising yoga at home. I wanted to know what was happening with me. I told Juan that for one hour a day I wanted a room for myself where I could be alone. He was very annoyed and accused me of being selfish wanting a room to myself, but I insisted. After all it was just for one hour a day. I was working hard but I got up at six o'clock each day so that I could prepare things in advance and I was always finished by one thirty, with the table set and the dinner ready. In that way I could keep the afternoons free so that I could read and spend some time alone, thinking.

Then one day I began to work for a woman who had broken her leg and needed a cleaner for a month, until she was back on her feet. She was a very nice woman and would sit on the sofa chatting to me while I worked. She told me about a yoga group she attended and invited me to go with her every Friday at six o'clock. One day she asked me what I would really like to do with my life and after a moment's thought I replied: "Become a teacher of yoga." As I said it I realised that this was very important to me. She told me about a course in Barcelona so I went along and enrolled;

they gave you the first class free so that you could be sure it was what you wanted. I loved it and I went to the class two days a week and continued working three days a week with my friend. I was now very happy with my life and how things were going but my friend saw it differently. One day when we were working together I began to tell her about my course and how much I was enjoying it when she turned on me and demanded to know who I thought I was and what I thought I was doing. I was stunned. I could see she was frustrated over something but I didn't know what it was and she refused to talk to me about it, so in the end I just said:

"I'm Paloma and I want to do this."

It was sad because she didn't want my friendship anymore.'

With her sons grown up the family had made one more move, back to Málaga, where they live together in a house that they have bought between them. Paloma still works as a cleaner but now spends more and more of her time teaching yoga.

Sex Education

Sex education has been slow to appear in schools. The "Organic Law of the Right to Education" that appeared in the Constitution of 1985 gave autonomy to schools and more freedom to teachers, including the freedom to introduce sex education if so desired. By 1991 the law explicitly defended and reiterated the need for sex education within schools at different grades. It was considered to promote attitudes of gender equality and to discourage discrimination between the sexes. However it was not very systematic in its approach and did not lay down specific guidelines for the teachers, who not having received any training or support in this subject, tended to shy away from it. Informal methods of putting the message across, a Ministry of Health campaign designed to prevent unwanted pregnancies and adult television programmes, such as "We Speak of Sex", have had better results. But even these drew complaints from the Church. A government campaign to promote condoms to prevent the spread of AIDS caused condemnation from a Church that still frowned upon contraception and taught that not only was it illegal, it was also immoral.

During Franco's time the Church dominated attitudes to sex and indoctrinated the children in their schools as to its evils, labelling the penis as the "diabolical serpent" and the vagina as "Satan's den".

JUANA ISABEL born in MONTIJO in 1960

Juana Isabel (Juanibel) was born in Montijo, Extramadura. She is married to a doctor, has no children and works at the local hospital as a midwife. She came to Málaga after she completed her training and has lived there ever since.

Juanibel is a midwife at the local hospital; she is a slim, vibrant young woman with enormous brown eyes that she uses with great skill to accentuate her every word.

'I've always liked looking after people; I'm a good carer and I've always been interested in the health service. My father would have preferred me to study law, like my two brothers but I didn't want to. Maybe I was just being contrary. For my father it was fundamental that I had a good education and he sent me to an excellent boarding school; it was over a hundred kilometres from where we lived but it was the best around. It was run by the nuns and was for girls only but there was a boys' boarding school in the same village and my brother, Paco, went there. We both started when we were nine years old and we have a laugh now when we remember those days; on Sundays the boys who had sisters in the girls' school were allowed to visit them. Can you imagine him at nine years old, in his jacket and tie and me in my school uniform, only a year older, sitting there chatting like two old people. I wonder now what on earth we talked about. But I suppose it was some contact with the family because we weren't allowed to go home every weekend like you can nowadays. Not that I minded because I loved boarding school, but Paco took a little while to get used to it; he cried a lot at first. He was always a bit of a mother's boy. Even when he was older he would say that his mother was the best in the world and he wanted his wife to be just like his mother.

I remember once when my parents went to his school for prize giving he spotted them from an upstairs window and started shouting: *"La madre más guapa!"*, "The most beautiful mother." My mother was too embarrassed to get out of the car.

I studied for my Baccalaureate for six years then transferred to a mixed Jesuit school to do my two years preparation for university; the choice was between arts and science, pure or applied. I was actually better at the arts but I chose applied science, in particular health science. I went to university a year earlier than usual, at seventeen, and when I qualified I applied to the *Instituto de Salud* for a job. Job applications are assessed in terms of the points you have been awarded according to your qualifications, the results of your exams and your experience and my first posting as a midwife was to a hospital near Zafra where I stayed for two years. Then I started looking for a transfer; I applied for Seville, Málaga and Veléz Málaga. I fancied Seville because I love the city but I was also very interested in Málaga because it was one of the few hospitals where the midwives have a wider range of duties. In most hospitals the midwives only handled the births; any other problems or complications such as diabetes or high blood pressure were handled by nurses. In Málaga the midwives were involved with the whole range of complications that can happen during the pregnancy and the birth. For me this was a really interesting because I was trained to cope with these situations and in Málaga I would have the experience of doing so. The first vacancy that came up was in Velez Málaga and as that was not far from Málaga I accepted it, thinking that I would stay a year then ask for a transfer to Málaga. In fact I have been there ever since because I enjoy the working atmosphere in the hospital; it's almost twenty years now,' she added.

I asked her if she had seen many changes in that time.

'Oh yes, lots of changes in the way we do things. Women used to suffer from high blood pressure and other problems relating to the pregnancy much more than they do now. But the main thing is that nowadays the woman controls her pregnancy unlike before when there were lots of unwanted pregnancies. The entire process is much better controlled and the mother is in charge of her body and the birth of her child. Before there was a great deal of ignorance about what was happening; women didn't understand their sexuality or their bodies.

The average woman coming to the maternity ward for the first time is also much older than before; women today want to finish their studies, buy a house, furnish it and generally have a stable situation before they decide to have a baby. The average age of a mother giving birth for the first time was between twenty-two and twenty-four, now it's more like thirty-two to thirty-four. Of course now we see more foreigners coming into to the hospital, especially in this area, being so near to the coast; there are English, German, Rumanian, Eastern European and Moroccans.

I have some difficulty understanding the Arab women who come in, not so much their language but their behaviour; it is very different. They all seem to have a very low pain threshold and sometimes when I hear them screaming I rush in expecting the baby to be on its way and it is nothing. It really bothers me; I think someone should do a study on this. It's my personal opinion that the Arab woman generally has such a lowly position in her household that when she is pregnant for once in her life she has some importance and she wants to make the most of it. But that's only my opinion.

There is a lot of controversy about the various trends we have now in childbirth. Before there was no choice on the manner in which you had your baby; everyone followed the same strict protocols. Now a woman can ask for what she wants. In Marbella, which has a higher social level than here in Velez, the mother is given a menu to choose exactly how she would like the birth to go; it's actually called *el menu del parto*, menu of the birth. She can decide whether to wear a hospital gown or her own clothes, to have the child with her at all times, which drugs she wants, whether to have a caesarean, whether to break her waters or wait, the involvement of the father, in fact every stage of the birth process. They even have the facilities for the mother to have her baby in a birthing pool. We have one planned for this hospital,' she added. 'They are building a new maternity wing which should be ready by 2010 and that will have a birthing pool.

Actually I am a bit of reactionary; I'm not really in agreement with such a wide choice for the mother because when it comes down to it she does not really know what is best for her; she can't; she hasn't the experience or the training. It's all to do with fashion anyway. Nowadays most people say they want the most natural birth possible but often situations arise where they need our intervention. Sometimes this can be a problem; for example with a natural birth they can eat and drink normally, but then if they have a problem and the doctor has to anaesthetise them there is a greater risk. And of course if anything goes wrong we in the hospital are to blame and the parents will sue us; our problem is that we have no protocol to protect us from this.

Lots of women come in saying they want a natural birth then when the pain starts they ask for an epidural; well that's not a natural birth. Many women are not well informed; they are manipulated by fashion and what they read in the magazines. I believe that they should be able to say what they want to up to a point but they have to realise that they cannot expect to know as much as the midwife just because they have attended eight pre-natal classes and read a few books. I consider I am at the height of my profession: I'm very experienced but I'm still young, my reflexes are excellent and I have a clear mind. I don't think it matters what the fashion is as long as the birth is quick and the mother and baby are well.

The politics today say that midwives should not intervene in the birth; well I'm open to new ideas but I would like to see some evidence to back up these ideas and there isn't any. A birth with no intervention is usually slow and painful and the mother can be in labour for many hours. The other day my boss was attending the daughter of a friend who wanted a natural childbirth but had also asked for an epidural. She had been in labour for a long time and nothing was happening. I said to my boss that if this had been ten years ago the woman would have had her baby by now. We waited a bit longer then I suggested she remove the epidural so that the woman could feel the pain of the contractions and push otherwise we would still be there at Christmas. At last she agreed with me and we delivered the baby safely in the traditional way.

I always ask my patients when they reach a certain point in their labour how they would like to proceed; whether they want to wait and let the birth happen spontaneously or whether they would like me to help them. By that stage most mothers say they would like it to be over as soon as possible and are grateful for my help. They say that natural childbirth is stress free but I can't see it; if the birth is long and painful it induces much more stress in the mother and the baby. I am a bit old-fashioned in this respect; I think it is best for everyone if the birth is quick and not too painful.

There is always some new trend; now we have these birthing stools so that the mother can be vertical when her baby is born. They are fine as long as they don't want the midwife to sit on the floor and help.'

She grabbed a cushion and sat on the floor in front of me, indicating where the mother would be on the stool and where the midwife would have to sit.

'Sometimes the mother is in labour for hours and needs my help. Am I expected to sit here like this all that time? And then when the baby arrives if I am sitting there to deliver it all the fluids from the birth pour right over me. No thank you. I have my rights as well. They can use the birthing stool and hand me the baby as soon as it's born if they wish but I am not sitting down there for the birth.'

She stood up and resumed her seat before continuing:

'Lots of the changes are good, for example the mothers have weeks of pre-natal care from the midwife at their local health centre. She does initial health checks on blood pressure, weight and general health and then she runs a series of classes to explain everything: breathing and relaxation techniques, the sorts of tests they will have to do to check that the baby is alright, the birth itself and how to look after the baby when it is born. The fathers are asked to attend to give their wives support and so that they feel involved in the birth. She also brings her whole class to the hospital so that they see where their babies will be born and will not feel so strange when they have to come themselves. Then when the child is born the midwife visits them at home to check that everything is alright. There's usually no problem because most women leave the hospital and go straight to their mother or mother-in-law for a few weeks.

The fathers can also be present at the birth if they wish;

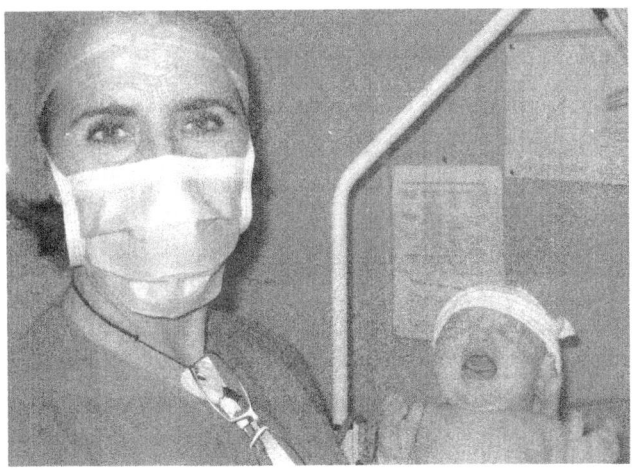

they help their wife through the labour and they even cut the umbilical cord when the baby is born. That's something that never happened before; when I was born my father never even went into the room until I had arrived. You didn't in those days; the men left it to the women.

I was born at home and a midwife and a doctor came to the house. People forget that many women died in childbirth in those days; both my aunt and my grandmother died giving birth. Childbirth is still dangerous; when a woman starts to bleed she can be dead in ten minutes; I would be frightened to work like that. That's why I think it is safest to have a baby in the hospital not at home. In Spain almost all births are hospital births, although there is a small movement towards home births, about one percent.

Years ago people were very worried when someone was about to give birth because they never knew if the mother and child would survive the experience, today it is a cause for celebration. Women arrange to go to the hairdressers the day before they go into hospital so that they can look their best for the photographs and visitors and all their family come to see them. Sometimes it's like a party in the maternity ward. Today nobody accepts that there could be any risk in giving birth so if anything does go wrong and there are complications it is always blamed on the hospital. There are lots of complaints. I say: "You may want a menu of the birth but I want a menu of the help I can give you." Births take much longer than before and people are starting to comment on it.'

'Tell me some more about your family,' I said.

'Well I have two brothers and a sister; I'm the eldest. We all studied hard; for people of my generation it was fundamental to study, even women. When my mother was young women normally only had a very basic education and never thought about going to work; my mother never worked and only one of her friends did; actually she was a midwife too. My father didn't have much of an education either because his father was killed in the Civil War when he was ten and his mother had to look after him and his sister. But my father had a *Butano* gas delivery service and became a successful businessman and he was very keen for all his children to study and have good careers.

My mother had a sad childhood. As I mentioned earlier her mother died in childbirth and so she was brought up by a widowed aunt from Valladolid. The aunt was a young woman and she moved to Montijo to live in the same house as my grandfather, who had an electricity business and helped him to take care of my mother. My grandfather, Antonio, had loved his wife very much but he decided to marry the aunt because it did not look good for them to live in the same house together and not be married. The aunt was a rather temperamental woman and liked everything to be done perfectly, so she was very strict with my mother. My mother's friends used to taunt her saying that the aunt didn't love her because she wasn't her real mother and this really upset my mother. It took her many years to understand that her aunt did love her and it caused her a lot of trauma when she was growing up, causing her to develop a pattern of insomnia that has stayed with her all her life. As an older woman she became very fond of the aunt, who lived with my parents all their married life. My father loved her too; she helped keep their home well organised and she was an excellent cook. When I was born my mother called me after both my grandmother, whose name was Juana and the aunt who was called Isabel.

When I first moved to Málaga I rented a flat with a girlfriend; my father didn't mind me moving away because by then, 1989, it was quite normal for women to live away from home. Then I met my husband, who is a paediatrician, through a friend of his who was a gynaecologist at my hospital. My father was not very pleased when we said we were getting married because my husband was divorced; both my parents thought I could do better for myself than marry a divorced man. But in the end there was no real problem and they soon became very fond of him.'

Contraception

In 1964 the first packet of the contraceptive pill arrived in Spain, where it was at first only prescribed on medical grounds. Gradually its use became more widespread and by 1975 it was being used by over half a million women. Even after Franco's death, when the sale of the contraceptive pill was no longer illegal, it still was not a simple thing to acquire; many pharmacists refused to sell it on moral grounds and many doctors refused to prescribe it. As late as 1989 a survey revealed that the most common method of contraception was still withdrawal, followed by the Pill, the sheath and lastly the Rhythm Method; the influence of the Church and the prohibition of the Franco era still lingered on. However as in other European countries, the emergence of this simple contraceptive pill had an enormous effect on the lives of women all over the country.

PAOLA born in Portugal in 1952

Paola is the owner of a Spanish language school in Málaga. She has run her own business for twenty-two years. She is divorced and has one daughter. She was born in Portugal and moved to Spain when she was twelve years old.

I had met Paola back in the late eighties when I had first come to Spain. I needed to learn Spanish in a hurry and I leafed through the Yellow Pages until I found a suitable language school, the *Escuela Cervantes*. I chose it because I liked the name and because it was not too far from where I lived. Paola was the owner and principal teacher of the school; she wrote all the teaching materials, marketed the courses, did most of the administration and taught the students. Admittedly she had a few staff to help her but it was Paola who was the driving force and everyone, staff and pupils alike, was terrified of her. Being nearer to her age than many of the other pupils, she and I soon became friends. We even struck up a bargain where I received extra classes in return for teaching her English; this agreement veered heavily in my favour as she was often too busy to have her English class and never did any homework.

Today Paola still has her language school and is still heavily committed to all she does. She took up the tale where her mother, Araceli, had left off:

'Well as my mother said, I was born in Portugal and didn't move to Spain until I was twelve. I was an only child; everyone says I was a quiet child but very restless, always on the go. My parents were very strict with me and very protective; when I was a child they would never let me leave the house on my own.

I was sent to a good school and I was a hard-working student because I liked learning and didn't find it difficult, but I was always in trouble for talking. Our teacher was very strict; she had an ebony ruler and would hit you on the hand with it for any small misdemeanour. My mother never had any sympathy for me; she would encourage the teacher to hit me if I was naughty.'

As she said this she looked sidewise at her mother and I felt that this memory still rankled. Araceli ignored her and continued eating the muscatel grapes from the dish.

'The children in the class were divided into three groups: the clever ones, the average ones and the naughty ones. One of the punishments which I absolutely hated was to be put in the bottom group for misbehaving. I would sooner have been hit with the ruler. But despite all that, I liked my teacher; she was a good teacher and taught me a lot.'

At this point Araceli declared she was tired and was going back to her own flat. I got up to kiss her goodbye and thanked her for her help and Paola escorted her to the door. Then she came back and resumed what she had been saying. She looked noticeably more relaxed now that her mother had left.

'I don't know if you know but in 1961 Portugal became involved in a long drawn-out war against its African colonies and things became much more difficult living there, so after a few years we moved to Madrid. I was twelve at the time. My parents sent me to a private school, but not a religious one and I began to study for my Baccalaureate; the school was mixed but the boys and girls were taught separately. That period in Madrid was a bad time for me. We lived in the house of an uncle, who was a horrible man; he abused his wife and son badly. I was a very impressionable child and it affected me a lot; I became very angry with my mother because she ignored how I felt. She just did not consider my feelings at all.'

Her eyes were shiny with unshed tears as she said this and it was obvious that the resentment against her mother still smouldered.

'Then we moved to Extramadura to stay with my grandparents in a small village called Casa de Don Pedro and life began to get better for me. It was the first time I had had any freedom; it was totally different from living in a big city and I was allowed to go out whenever I wanted. I loved my grandparents, especially my grandmother. My parents wouldn't send me to the local school; they employed a private teacher so that I could continue with my studies for the Baccalaureate.

Then when I was fourteen we moved to Málaga. I had a lot of friends, many of them very religious, and we used to go out in a group together. I went to Mass, we all did in those days, but apart from that I was not involved with the church. We had to cover our hair with scarves before going into the church and no bare arms or legs were allowed or the priest would tell you off. There was another group of older women that I was friendly with as well and we went to the dances together. I remember that two or three of them were teachers, one was the daughter of a chemist and the other was the sister of the mayor. I had a lot more freedom with them. I began to use make-up and I even coloured my hair with water and bleach.

That was when I started to form my personal ideas on independence and relationships; I had three things very clear in my mind: I wasn't going to marry except for love, I would not tolerate my husband beating me, and I would always be financially independent. In fact I achieved all of them; I never had to worry about my husband's reaction if he had to wait for me to come home to cook the dinner and I've always managed to earn my own money, so I never had to ask him for anything.

Anyway after I had passed my Baccalaureate, instead of going straight to university, I went to Switzerland to learn French. First of all I went to live with the sister-in-law of a friend of my mother's and looked after her children, but that didn't last very long. I preferred my independence so I decided to look for a place of my own. It was not usual for young Spanish women to go abroad unaccompanied at that time; in fact not many people travelled outside of Spain at all. It was a great culture shock for me and I had to adapt my ideas rather quickly. It was the era of the hippies, which of course arrived in Spain much later than the rest of the world. For me it was a cultural revelation; I made friends with some very interesting women, not Swiss, mostly Latin women from Costa Rica, South America and the States. I enjoyed being there, going to bars, restaurants, dances and of course learning the language; I learnt a lot of French.

Then when I returned to Málaga I went to university. In those days there were always fewer women than men in the universities, except in my subject, Literature and Language. Franco died whilst I was at university and then things began to change a lot. The students in the universities began to fight for democracy but I didn't get caught up in any of it; I didn't really want to mix with that kind of student. I went to the parties but I never really became part of the scene; I didn't like their life style, smoking pot and free love. They were too modern for me; I was much more conservative in my attitudes.

It was about this time that I went through a crisis of faith, against the church, against everything. In those days I was a very passionate girl; I became angry with the people who governed the church, even the Pope. I also began to doubt in the existence of God. Nowadays I do believe in God but I don't like to ask too many questions; I don't want my doubts to return. If I'm honest I suppose it's a selfish need to have something to believe in. My daughter also went through a similar crisis when she declared she didn't believe in God anymore but she was much younger, only eight years old. I think it was to do with the death of her father when she was very young. I haven't tried to influence her one way or the other; I think she has to make her own mind up about God. I remember when she became old enough to take her first communion I said nothing and just waited to see what she would decide. In the end she joined her friends and they all took their first communion together. She's not a practising Catholic but she goes to church occasionally, usually on special occasions such as Christmas and Easter.

When I finished my degree I took a job in administration, but I didn't really like it; I wanted to teach in a language school. I had a friend who worked in the only language school in Málaga that taught Spanish for foreigners and one day she told me there was a vacancy. I was very lucky to get the job and I just loved it; I really enjoyed the contact with the students, I prepared my lessons and designed work books for them. You have to remember that in those days people in Spain knew very little about life in other countries, so I was fascinated to meet all these foreigners and learn about where they had come from and what their lives were like.

I didn't have any thoughts about running my own school then, but events just led to it. The owner of the school was a drunk and a gambler. When you went to get paid he'd have your wages in the drawer and a bottle of cognac on his desk. The staff didn't have any contracts; there was no organisation; it was a shambles; everything was left to the individual teacher. One day he collapsed and was taken to hospital. His wife was distraught; she knew nothing about business and she asked me and another teacher to take over the running of the school. It soon became obvious that the wife was only interested in taking money out of the business and didn't want to invest anything in it, so after a couple of years we decided to set up our own school. I rented a site and one Easter I went abroad to look for students. I opened my school in 1987 with one group of students and me.

Paola welcoming her new students

I met my husband, Paco, in Málaga where he had a law practice. I was friendly with one of his colleagues and he introduced me to Paco on two or three occasions, but at first I wasn't particularly interested; I thought he was too dry and serious. Then about two or three years later I was in this café with a girlfriend and suddenly she said: "I like that man; he's so dignified and elegant. There's something special about him." I looked across to where she was pointing and it was him; he was standing at the bar talking to some friends. He had been out on the boat with us that day and I'd ignored him. Now I found myself seeing him in a different way and when he spoke to me on his way to the cigarette machine, I became a bit friendlier towards him. My friend invited him to join us the next day on the boat and after that I started going out with him.

We went out together as *novios* for six years before we got married. We never lived together, nor slept together; it was still frowned upon even then. Besides which I wanted to marry in a church, in white with a veil and all the usual things. I remember that I didn't expect to be emotional at my wedding, but when we came out of the church and I saw my father I hugged him and began to cry and cry.

We didn't want a child straight away so I took the pill. This was 1980 and Franco was dead so by then the sale and use of contraceptives was legal. We waited two years then I stopped taking the pill and little Paola was conceived the next month.'

To distinguish between them her daughter is usually referred to as *Paola pequeño,* although she is now a tall, willowy twenty-five year old.

'By then my life with Paco was becoming complicated and I had to work longer hours, so when Paola was born we didn't even consider having any more children. In fact it wasn't long after that that we separated. Then two years later Paco died from a heart attack.'

She stopped and poured out some more water.

'Tell me about little Paola. How did her life differ from yours at the same age?' I asked her as she obviously did not want to talk any more about her husband.

'Oh well, there are lots of differences: she is much more independent, freer and can choose what she wants to do. In my generation your parents were parents, not friends. If they said no, that was it. Now if I say no to Paola I have to give an explanation. We communicate a lot more. In the early years I was a mother to Paola then I was both a mother and a father, then much later, I became a friend. Strangely though, she is much more conservative in her attitudes than I am.

But children today expect a lot more; there is much more money to spend on them and they expect the latest toys and fashions and brand names. None of that existed in my day. Her friends can visit the house or call for her to go out; in my time many of my friends wanted to have a boyfriend because it was the only way to get out of the house without your parents. But then once you had a boyfriend you weren't expected to go out with your friends anymore. Actually I was a bit different in that respect; I would never give up my girlfriends for a boyfriend. And of course if you got pregnant you had to marry straight away.

I was always clear on that point; I would never get pregnant while I was single and if by some mishap I did, I would never marry the father because I wouldn't want him accusing me of wanting to be pregnant. It's always the woman's fault,' she added bitterly.

'Even though contraception was legal by then it was not easy to buy the pill; it depended on the doctor and the chemist. Some would refuse to sell it to you. Of course it was much more difficult in the villages where everyone knew everyone else. There were hardly any single mothers in those days because they knew that unless they got married their families would throw them out on the street. It was virtually impossible to get an abortion in Spain so lots of girls in Málaga went to London. There were special trips just for that; "*Viajes Preparados*" they were called, "Package Holidays".

Once, a very good friend of mine wanted an abortion. She told nobody except me and begged me to go to London with her to have it done. We told her family that we were going to Granada to a friend's house and booked two flights to London; it was very difficult to get away without anyone knowing. My friend didn't book a "*Viaje Preparado*" so when we arrived in London we didn't know where to go or what to do. We had no appointment and no address. We got on an open-top tourist bus and we asked the conductor where we could find an abortion clinic and he gave us the name and address of a doctor straight away, just like that. I am against abortion and I was very much against her having one but she was adamant and in the end I was the only one who could go with her. Even today I am the only person who knows about it.'

Abortion

Despite the ease with which people can now access a variety of methods of contraception and the generally open attitude towards sex and sex education, the number of abortions continued to rise until 2009 when, at first, it dropped and then became steady. According to a Spanish Health Ministry report the abortion rate rose from 49,367 in 1995 to 115,812 in 2008 but only increased to 118,359 by 2011. Part of the reason for this was the easy availablity of over-the-counter medicines such as "the morning after pill".

Designated a crime during Franco's rule, abortion was not made legal until 1985 when the law allowed for the termination of pregnancy in certain cases: where it was the result of a rape, if a foetus of up to twelve weeks was malformed and where the birth would lead to the mental or physical health of the mother being endangered. Most abortions were for the latter. The lack of abortion facilities during the Franco years meant that many women went abroad to clinics in Harley Street in London to have their pregnancies terminated. Almost always this was a recourse used by the wealthy; nevertheless in 1978 over fourteen thousand Spanish women went to London for abortions.

In 2010 the 1985 Law was reformed and abortion was permitted in any circumstances up to the first fourteen weeks, if there was risk to the mother or child's health up to 22 weeks and if the baby had any abnormalities. Girls between sixteen and seventeen were allowed to have an abortion without their parents' consent. When the new law was passed, a million protestors took to the streets of Madrid to demonstrate their objections.

In 2013, Spain's conservative government approved a law to ban abortion except in cases of rape or where the mother's health was at risk and all abortions had to receive approval from two independent doctors. It was not permitted to abort a foetus because of signs of abnormalities. This proposed amendment to Law 2/2010 has been met with a great deal of opposition and has not yet been approved.

REMEDIOS born in Almogia in 1953

Remedios was born in Almogia, where she has lived all her life. She works in Málaga as a maid/housekeeper and is unmarried with one son.

My first visit to Almogia was at Christmas time in the late eighties. A good friend of mine, a German woman who had moved to Spain when she was twenty one and married a Spaniard, told me that her maid, Remedios, wanted to show me her house and had invited us to eat with her family. I had tasted Remedios's cooking before, so did not have to be asked twice.

To the casual visitor Almogia appears to be in the middle of nowhere, although it is actually only twenty five kilometres north of Málaga, up a steep and torturously winding road. Twenty years ago, the road was a series of sharp bends, with the mountain face on one side and a sheer drop on the other. Today the worst of the bends have been straightened out and crash barriers installed, but the land either side still has a uniform covering of coarse scrub, almond trees and olives. The bleak and bare limestone outcrops of the high ground contrast vividly with the deep red soil below.

Even in December the sun was hot and strong and we drove with the car windows open, breathing in the dry air, redolent with the smell of thyme, lavender and rosemary. The first sight of the pueblo came as a surprise, for out of the seemingly deserted mountains, as we rounded yet another bend in the road, there was Almogia, glistening white before us. It seemed a town from another time, another land. There appeared to be no reason for its existence in that remote place; we had passed no buildings, save a solitary *venta,* since we had left Málaga. There was little evidence of horticultural activity, only the olives and the almonds, growing unattended, and we had seen no people at all. In fact as I was soon to discover, Almogia had a thriving population made up of farmers and people who worked in a small co-operative, manufacturing clothing.

My delight at reaching the pueblo was only tempered by the prospect of having to return once more by the same nightmarish route. My companion directed us through a maze of narrow streets, squeezing past parked cars until we came to Remedios' house. We must have stood out as strangers to the pueblo because as we passed people stopped what they were doing and stared at us; even a group of old men, sitting outside the bar, enjoying the winter sunshine, interrupted their conversation to examine us closely.

Remedios had a house next door to her parents and younger brother. The houses, identical to all the others in the pueblo, were cut from stone and piled up together, like so many white boxes. The walls were a metre thick and the doorway low and narrow. She was delighted to see us and after the usual effusive welcome, ushered us into her house.

We stepped into a darkened room, welcoming the caress of the coolness after the bright sunshine outside. I could hardly believe what I saw before me. We had stepped out of a Moorish pueblo and into a richly decorated Málaga flat. A large, highly polished sideboard stood against one wall, a velour covered sofa and chairs were arranged opposite it. There were silver dishes, family photographs in gilt frames, glass vases, soft cushions, artificial flowers, thick brocade curtains and a glass coffee table.

'Remi was given the furniture when my husband's mother died,' whispered my friend by way of explanation. 'We didn't need it in our small apartment.'

I made appropriate noises of appreciation to a delighted Remedios, who then insisted I make a tour of inspection. The lower part of the house compromised of the room we had entered directly through the front door and a small alcove that served as a kitchen. A narrow, marble staircase led up to the bedrooms. The main bedroom was filled with a gigantic double bed, obviously from the same source as the rest of the furniture and was covered with a voluptuous blue silk quilt. Heavy curtains in matching blue silk hung at the tiny windows and above the bed was a small painting of the Virgin Mary. The second bedroom was tiny and belonged to her young son, José. The whole house glistened and gleamed and sparkled. The dry and dusty pueblo was carefully shut outside. We made our way downstairs, squeezing past each other and feeling distinctly too large and clumsy for this tiny, overcrowded home.

Through a narrow passage between the houses, that carried the imposing name of *Calle Murcia*, was a view of the mountains that dominate the landscape, bare and brown, but incredibly beautiful, and bathed in hot, bright sunlight. Standing there squinting from the unexpected glare, I felt that I could be somewhere in North Africa.

The tour was not over however.

'Would we like to see the turkey?' Remedios asked.

She led us through a ram-shackled shed at the side, past the rabbits in their cages and into an open space, or should I say, midden. The contrast could not have been starker: the gleaming, polished house on the one side and this smelly pile of rubbish where the turkey lived on the other. We stayed and admired the magnificent bird for as long as we could stand the flies and the stench. The turkey was not destined long for this world; his hour of glory was not far off because he was to be the main dish on the Night of the Kings, 5th January, when the family, along with the rest of Spain would have their main Christmas celebration.

The rabbits looked at us mournfully as we passed; no important feast for them, they would find themselves in a weekday stew, *estofado de conejo* or in Sunday's *paella*. A mongrel bitch, tied up with a length of rope, bared her teeth at us, daring us to venture near her or her pups. Everywhere we looked there were cats: tom cats, nursing mothers with their kittens, even a brand new litter with their eyes still unopened. Nobody seemed to know which kittens belonged to which cat.

At this point Remedios' parents appeared and smiled welcomingly as my friend introduced me. The father was a short, sprightly man, burnt brown by the sun. He seemed quite old, but was still working, buying and selling farm animals. The mother was dressed completely in black, after the fashion of widows and older women in Spain, and her long hair, still dark, was pulled back from her face and tied in a bun.

A widow could spend the rest of her life wearing black, but even women with husbands spent many years in black because of the strict rules of *luto*, the period of mourning. On the death of a spouse or child, the mourning period was two years, for a parent, one year, for a brother or sister it was six months and for other relatives such as uncles, aunts and cousins it was three months. With families of twelve and fourteen children as was not unusual in Franco's time, some women had barely packed away their black clothes before they needed them again. They were not allowed to attend any fiestas, weddings or general celebrations until the mourning period was over.

Remedios' mother stepped forward to kiss me, welcoming me to her pueblo. Her wrinkled face was wreathed in smiles, revealing a solitary tooth. She did not have much money she said, but what food and drink she had she would share with us.

'*Mi casa es tu casa*,' she said with typical Andalusian hospitality.

We were to eat in the parents' house, which had more space, although Remedios would prepare the food in her own kitchen then bring it round. She was determined to impress us; the food was typical of the region: local smoked ham, large plates of glistening olives, gazpacho soup and paella. The meal was washed down with copious glasses of local wine and we rose from the table feeling full, sleepy and in decidedly good spirits. Fear of the road home seemed to have evaporated. However there was more to follow and as we returned to Remedios's parlour we found the table was now set with the traditional Christmas sweetmeats: a large gilt dish contained a colourful selection of almonds, *turrón*, walnuts, raisins, and little biscuits wrapped in silver foil. While these were being handed out Remedios was pouring the champagne; not French champagne, but the equally delicious Spanish cava.

Life in the village had changed little since Franco's days and attitudes were vastly different from those in the bustling city of Málaga. Remedios had started working for my friend when she was only fourteen; she lived in their house, cooked three meals a day for them, washed and ironed their clothes, cleaned the house and helped to look after my friend's three small sons. Once a week she caught a local bus and went back to her pueblo to see her family. Everything was fine until she discovered she was pregnant. Her father was horrified; he told her she had dishonoured the family and forbade her to ever return to the family home. She and her baby son went to live with her sister and her sister's family in a one-bedroom flat in Málaga and she continued to work for my friend, taking the baby with her. However life was not easy for either of the sisters in such cramped conditions and they often quarrelled.

My friend watched as Remedios struggled with her new life and in the end she lost patience. With Teutonic forthrightness she said:

'This is ridiculous. This situation cannot continue any longer. I'm taking you home to Almogia.'

She packed Remedios and the baby into her car and drove them to the pueblo. Remedios's father was eating his lunch when they arrived. My friend marched into his house, carrying the baby, with Remedios a few steps behind.

'Here is your grandson,' she said and put the baby into his unsuspecting arms.

The man froze and said nothing as the tiny infant was thrust into his lap. A moment or two passed and he stood up and gave the child to his wife. Without speaking to anyone he turned and went out, leaving his unfinished lunch on the table.

'Shall we go after him?' asked Remedios.

'No, let him be for a bit. He has a lot to think about,' replied my friend.

Remedios's mother prepared them some lunch, then when they had finished, my friend said:

'OK. Let's go and find your father now.'

They picked up the baby and went to look for him. They found him with his donkey in a nearby field. Once more my friend went up to him, put the child in his arms and said:

'Here's your grandson.'

This time the man didn't put the child down; he held him for a few minutes then turned and sat him on the back of his donkey. My friend smiled at Remedios and left them. She walked back to her car and drove home to Málaga.

From that day the baby was an accepted member of the family; her mother looked after him while Remedios, who never married, continued to work for my friend.

Prostitution

A traditional male view of a woman was to place her in one of two categories: a mother or a whore. An unmarried woman who had sex or became pregnant dishonoured her father and her family and in many cases was forced to leave her family home. Very often the only way she and her child could survive was to turn to

prostitution.

A woman was expected to remain a virgin until she married, but there was no such restriction on a man. In fact men were expected to learn about sex through visiting the local brothel; a survey undertaken in the mid sixties showed that two thirds of all Spanish men had their first sexual encounter with a prostitute. Even in Franco's era, when censorship was at its worst, a law making brothels illegal was not introduced until 1956 and never implemented. By the time of his death there were half a million prostitutes in Spain.

Nowadays the prostitutes that advertise in all the daily papers and operate out of neon-lit, roadside brothels are mostly immigrants: Rumanian, Russian or Colombian girls lured to Spain with promises of work. Many former Spanish prostitutes have taken up government training initiatives to make career changes and now work for local government departments, a clear indication that their previous work was more from necessity than choice.

LOLA was born in Puente Genil in 1944

Lola is divorced with four children and two grandchildren. She never worked and for forty years was dominated by her husband who stole all her money and kept her without friends and family contact. She now lives alone in a rented apartment and her only income is a disability pension.

I arranged to meet Lola in the restaurant after she had finished playing golf. She was a smartly dressed woman of sixty-five; her reddish blonde hair was shoulder length and waved. She had obviously been an attractive woman and still retained some of her early beauty. I ordered a coffee and we began to talk. She was born in Puente Genil, a market town in the province of Cordoba. Her father owned a brick factory and was able to provide well for his six children; Lola was the penultimate.

'My father made sure all his children were well educated, even the girls. We were a big family: four girls and two boys. I enjoyed school and studied hard. When I passed my Baccalaureate I wanted to go to Madrid to university but my father would not hear of it. I begged and pleaded with him; I suggested he send me to a university for girl boarders but he still would not agree. No daughter of his was going to go to Madrid on her own. So I did what studying I could in Puente Genil; I went to classes of embroidery and I learnt to sew and use a sewing machine. It was interesting but not what I wanted to do.

Then when I was twenty I met my husband. I was so fed up with not being able to study or do anything worthwhile that I agreed to marry him after only three months. My father did not like him very much but he agreed to the wedding. My husband's family were from the higher classes of society but they had no money; he lived with his mother in Tarragona. When we were married we moved in with his mother. I was not very happy; my husband did no work and just sat around the house all day. Then I heard that they were looking for people to go to Switzerland to work so I persuaded my husband that we should go. We worked there for two years; he was a cook and I was a waitress in the same hotel. While we were there I became pregnant with my first child and when my parents heard the news my father sent for me. He bought me a house in Puente Genil and he gave my husband a job in his factory. That was our life for quite a few years and it would have been happy except for the fact that my husband was insanely jealous. I was not allowed to leave the house on my own; I could not even visit my sister or my friends. He would come from work to pick me up and take me to do the shopping then take me home again. After our second child was born I said I needed a car to take the children to school. He allowed me to do that but he would telephone to make sure I had gone straight home after dropping them off. He controlled me with the telephone. He was obsessed with the thought that I might be having an affair with someone; he was even suspicious of my brother-in-law. He once said that he loved me so much he wanted to cut himself open and sew me inside of him. That was not love; it was because he wanted to dominate me. But I was so blind in those days I thought that was what life was like. My mother had always been at home for us children so I didn't think my life was so different.

Then one day my husband went to see my mother and asked her if my parents had made a will. She told him that they had and that half the business was to go to her two sons and the remaining half was to be shared between the four girls. Somehow he persuaded her to change the will and give us all an equal share. I don't know how he did it but he was always a very persuasive talker and my mother agreed. She never told my father and when she died a couple of years later my father was shocked and angry to discover that the will had been altered. Then my husband told my father that he wanted my share of the inheritance there and then. I still don't understand why my father agreed but he gave him the monetary value of my share of the business. At first it wasn't too bad because he used it to buy his own brick factory in Puente Genil. Then he won some money on the lottery and he began to spend all his evenings and most of his days in the bars, buying drinks for all his friends. We never saw much of him as it was; he never ate with me and the children and now we saw even less of him. He was out all the time and didn't even bother to go into the factory. He had a manager who looked after everything for him. Well things went from bad to worse and then he decided we would move to Rincon de la Victoria to a flat that we had bought for the holidays. So we began to live there, right by the beach. Ever since I got married I had suffered from psoriasis and my doctor had said that the sea and the salt air would be good for it.

Life continued just as before; my husband was out all the time and I was left at home. When I went out with him I had to be careful not to look at any men because he would accuse me of wanting to have an affair with them; I would walk along with my eyes fixed on the ground. Then one day I was sitting on the beach with my children and some neighbours came up to me and started shouting. My husband had been trying to have a relationship with their sixteen year old daughter and they were very angry. I told them there was no point talking to me that they should speak to my husband. Anyway I was very upset about this and when he came home that night I said that I wanted to speak to him, somewhere where the children would not hear. So we went to a cafe and I told him what had happened. Of course he denied it all but the curious thing is that the next week he went out and looked for a new house; he sold our flat and bought a house at the far end of the town near the golf course, as far away as possible from the old flat.

By then he had so many debts and unpaid tax that he arranged for this new house to be in the name of our youngest son, Jorge, who was only about twelve at the time. I of course knew nothing of his financial problems because he would not let me see any papers or statements. I only found out about his debts each time I was expected to pay them.

It was when I began to live in this new house that my eyes started to be opened. I met women who lived normal lives; who went to the golf club to play with their friends; who stopped and had a drink with their friends; who did not live in fear of their husbands as I did. I began to realise that my life with Carlos was far from normal. It was also about this time that there were lots of articles in the press about abused wives and the associations that had been set up to help them.

I started to play golf and to socialise with our neighbours at the swimming pool but this made my husband even more jealous and his possessiveness took a nastier turn. He began to verbally abuse me, insulting me, calling me all sorts of ugly names and smashing plates and cups. One day a neighbour called to ask something, I don't remember what exactly. Carlos saw him standing in the doorway in his bathing trunks talking to me and he was furious. When the man had gone he began shouting at me, calling me a whore and other horrible names. I was very upset. To be called a whore when I had done nothing wrong and had been a faithful wife all those years. I can't tell you how much it hurt. That was when I told him to leave. He moved out and I changed the locks on the doors. I went to the police and I made a complaint against him but I could see that they did not really believe me; he had a lot of friends in the police force. But by now I was ready to end it; I found a solicitor and started divorce proceedings.

There were just two of us living at home then, Jorge and me; my other three children had all married and left home. One night my husband climbed up the back wall, over the balcony and came in through my son's open bedroom window. I was terrified and so was Jorge; we didn't know what he was going to do. He shouted a bit and threw some things around and then he left the way he had come. I made Jorge sleep with the windows closed after that. Then one day I came home and somehow he had got in and smashed up everything; there were broken bottles of wine, smashed china, broken furniture. It was awful. I telephoned the police again and this time when they saw the damage, they believed me. I took out a restraining order against him.

My husband moved to Tarragona to live with his mother and for the first time I began to feel relaxed. But he still would not leave us alone and continued to telephone Jorge and bit by bit he turned my son against me. Then I discovered that he had managed to get his hands on half my pension; it was being sent to his mother. I knew his mother was not receiving it so I telephoned his sister, who was and still is a good friend, and told her that either he sorted it out or I would make a complaint against his mother. The following month I received my full pension. But not for long. This was when I began to realise the full extent of his financial double-dealing. On many occasions he had made me sign bank papers without explaining what they were for. Now I realised that he had made me responsible for his debts. The tax office started deducting money from my pension to repay some of these debts and there was nothing I could do about it.

When my son became eighteen he turned to me and told me that the house we lived in was his and that I had to get out. I was very upset that he could treat me like that but I said: "Look Jorge you know that this is my house. It may be in your name but it's my house; it was my money that bought it. But I won't argue with you; I'll find somewhere to rent." So I rented an apartment on the same estate and four days later my ex-husband moved back into my house with Jorge. He had manipulated my son to get what he wanted. So now the two of them live in a house that was paid for with my money.

A little while later Jorge telephoned me to say that my car was also in his name and he wanted it or its value in cash. I needed the car so I borrowed the money and gave him four thousand euros. I just couldn't believe that my ex-husband would turn my son against me like that.

Anyway now I live alone and I am happy. For the first time in forty years I can relax and not worry about what my husband is going to think or say or do. My psoriasis has cleared up completely and my arthritis is in remission. I can go where I want when I want. It's wonderful. I gave forty years of my life to my children and my husband and now the rest of my life is for me.'

Domestic violence

Centuries of regarding their wives as chattels has meant that many men believed that they could treat them as they wished and this created a climate where domestic violence could flourish. During Franco's forty year rule, beating your wife was not considered a crime and although after the death of Franco women began to find it easier to escape from unhappy marriages there were still other areas where their rights were unequal. Before 1987 a female rape victim, unlike a victim of any other crime, was obliged to prove that she had fought "heroically" to defend herself against her attacker in order to be considered a genuine victim. It was not until the ruling from a Supreme Court trial in 1987 that a rape victim no longer had to prove she had tried to defend herself in order to be taken seriously. Even today the rape victim does not always receive justice. According to Montserrat Comas of the organisation Judges for Democracy, although many sentences for rape are severe, the laws on violence against women are imprecise and leave too much latitude for interpretation by individual judges.

Domestic violence as defined by the law is both physical and sexual; it includes insults, death threats and attempts to humiliate the victim. Economic violence and isolation, both attempts to control and exercise power over the victim, as experienced by Lola, are also forms of domestic violence.

It was not until 2004 that a new law, "Ley Orgánica 1/2004 de Medidas de Protección Integral contra la Violencia de Género" was passed to combat this. The law specifically referred to "gender violence", so that male victims were also included even though the majority of victims were women.

Within months over a thousand women had sought protection. The law gave a battered woman the opportunity to get a restraining order against her violent spouse within seventy-two hours; it became easier for victims to seek legal redress and it deemed particular aspects of domestic violence, such as death threats, to be crimes.

It had taken many years for the law to come onto the statute books despite many high-profile domestic violence cases, one of the most notable being of a sixty-year-old woman who had suffered years of beatings by her husband. In 1997 unable to get the police to help her or to issue a restraining order against her husband she appeared on a television show to denounce him for decades of brutal beatings; a few days later she was found dead. Her husband had beaten her yet again, poured petrol over her and set light to her. It was this brutal action that helped the government of the day to redefine domestic violence as a crime and not just a misdemeanour.

Since then the number of shelters has increased and the number of help desks has doubled. Today battered women can receive shelter and economic assistance; there are people to help them find work and become independent. But the number of incidents is still as shocking; in the first half of 2003 there were seventy-four deaths from domestic violence and a rise in the number of reported cases. According to the Federation of Separated and Divorced Women these increases were because women were at last beginning to confront their attackers, something which in turn could cause an upsurge in violence. In 2004 seventy-two women were killed, sixty-seven of them by their husbands and in 2010 seventy-three women died at the hands of their partners or spouses.

Although campaigners would like the new laws to go further, they are quick to point out that the main achievement has been in pulling domestic violence out of a closed, private area into the public domain. A popular Spanish film about domestic violence, "I Give You My Eyes", won the Spanish Oscar award, Las Goyas, in 2004. At last the subject was no longer taboo. However women are still reluctant to denounce their attackers and it is estimated that eight out of ten women do not report domestic violence. The government now gives high priority to tackling this issue but according to the Spanish Minister for Work and Social Affairs what is required is a change in behaviour towards women, something that will have to be tackled in the schools.

A charitable association called Asociación Aspacia, which is subsidised by the Health Ministry, is attempting to address the problem through the perpetrators of the violence rather than the victims, offering men the chance to have therapy and change their attitudes to women. However, some think it will take more than therapy to change Spain's well-entrenched machismo ideology.

CRISTINA born in Málaga in 1981

Cristina was born in Málaga and works there as a hairdresser. She is single and lives with boyfriend and his mother.

Cristina is a hairdresser and she lives with her boyfriend in his mother's house.

'It's very convenient. I've lived there for about a year now. My boyfriend's mother is very nice; I get on with her well. It would be nice to be more independent, but at least in this way we get the chance to save. Later we will look for our own place: a little flat nearby would be nice.

His mother is really kind to me; she treats me like a daughter. This morning for example, I didn't feel too well, so she made me some special tea to settle my stomach. She always has the meal ready when we get home from work, and she does the shopping and washes our clothes. I'm very lucky; I don't have to do anything. It's better than being in my own home. I think she likes the company because her husband's dead and she only has one son. Now she has me as a daughter too.

We've talked about getting married, but not for a while yet, probably when I'm thirty. Then I think we'll have a civil wedding. I don't believe in the church, so I don't see any point in getting married in church. If we ever do get married, I think I'd like to be married at La Conception, in the botanical gardens; it's really lovely there with all the trees and plants.

Not many of my friends want to get married; they prefer to live together. Life's so uncertain these days, what's the point in getting married if it's not going to last. One of my sisters is married, and so is one of my brothers, and the other sister is living with her boyfriend.

There are six of us in our family: three boys and three girls. I don't want to have so many children; I think two is plenty, but my boyfriend says he would just like one. That's because he's an only child and he doesn't know how much fun it is to have brothers and sisters. We all had such good times together when we were kids. Sometimes we stayed at my grandfather's farm in the country; that was great.

I remember once, my sister fell off her bike, so we covered her in the red petals of some plant that grew nearby, so that it looked like blood. We made her lie in the road next to her bike, covered in these petals and the rest of us hid in the bushes and waited for a car to come by. Sometimes it would take twenty minutes for a car to come, because it was a quiet lane. When the driver saw my sister lying in the road, he would get out and run up to her, really upset and then we would jump out of the hedge and laugh. We spent the whole day doing this.'

She laughed at the memory.

'We're a very close family. We usually all meet up at the weekends and do something together.'

The Family

Many people voiced concerns about the effects that easier divorce would have on the family. In fact the role and structure of the family has changed since the demise of Franco. Fewer young people are marrying and when they do marry they are older. Very often both partners work and if they decide to marry and have children they do so later in life than previously. The Spanish are abandoning the extended family that for centuries has held their society together and are embracing the nuclear family like the rest of Europe. Households with three or four generations living under the same roof now hardly exist. The average size of the Spanish family has dropped from 3.8 to 2.9 in the last thirty years and over two and a half million Spanish live alone. The population is declining and recent statistics indicate that Spain now has one of the lowest fertility rates in Europe. To combat this, the government has offered a financial incentive of 2,500 euros for every new child born and where there are already three or more children in the family a further 1,000 euros. To quote the prime minister, José Luis Zapatero: "In order to continue progressing Spain needs more families with more children. And families need more aid to have babies and more resources for their upbringing." Franco too had tried to encourage people to have more babies by offering financial incentives but he gave them to the fathers.

After Franco's death people were allowed to get married in a register office with a civil ceremony and were no longer obliged to have a full Catholic wedding in church. Some young Spaniards have abandoned the idea of marriage altogether and are happy to live together as a couple and even have children without the strictures of a marriage contract. This in part may be due to a greater participation by women in the work force but also to an increased desire for personal liberty and happiness on both parts. Woman are shrugging off the traditional role of self-sacrifice for the sake of the family and are looking for more personal satisfaction through combining the roles of mother and wage earner. Their partners, raised by more traditional mothers, often find it hard to adjust to this new style of woman, who expects them to not only share the job of wage-earner but also participate in the role of home-making. Often living together as partners is less complicated than marrying and can be seen to have an easier escape route if all goes wrong.

However despite these changes the emotional bond of the family holds strong and large family reunions are still commonplace, whether it be for a weekly Sunday lunch, birthdays, first communions or holidays. The concept of family is still very important to the Spaniards.

MARY LOLY was born in Málaga in 1956

Mary Loly is married and has one son. She works as a teacher in a private school.

Mary Loly was staying in her parents' summer house for the moths of July and August as she and her husband did every year.

'I was named after my mother, Maria Dolores, but I have always hated the name Dolores, *dolor*, pain; so people called me Lola, Loly, Mary Lo, now I'm Mary Loly.

Originally I wanted to study medicine and become a doctor, but my father knew it would not suit me and persuaded me against it. He knew that if I saw someone suffering and in pain I would suffer too; I can't help it. I wouldn't make a good doctor; I would get too involved, but I'm still very interested in anything to do with medicine.

Well one summer when I had finished school, I was about eighteen at the time, a neighbour came round and asked me if I would help her four year old son with his schoolwork. We were staying in this house at the time and he came round each day to see me. I discovered that I really enjoyed teaching this little boy so I decided I would become a teacher. I did a three year Teachers' Certificate and also studied English, French and Maths. I got good results in them all. I also studied Music: three years piano, five years theory and three years choral. I was very well qualified but when I went for a job I had a problem. To apply for a government teaching job you had to sit an entry exam and as I hadn't studied specifically for this exam, I failed it and didn't get accepted. However a cousin of my father was the head of a private school in Málaga and he offered me a job. I've been there ever since; it's now twenty-eight years since I started.

In those days there were few public schools and many private schools; nowadays most of the private schools are supported by the government and have been renamed *concertado*, grant aided. Originally the school paid my salary but now it's paid by the government and I have the same rights as a teacher in a public school.

I see quite a difference between when I started teaching at twenty-three years old and nowadays. My first class was with twelve to thirteen year olds. They were always so respectful, calling me *usted* and opening the door for me, but at the same time they felt able to come and talk to me about their problems. We had a very nice relationship. Then after I had been there about twelve years, in the early nineties, one of my colleagues retired and I applied for her job; she had taught the First Year, six year olds. I'm so glad I made that decision because now the twelve year olds are impossible to teach. It's not just that they no longer call me *usted* or that they call me Loly, it's because they have no respect at all for any of their teachers. Children know more about the world these days. Twelve year old girls today are like sixteen year olds with their earrings, body piercing, tattoos and of course their boyfriends. I have my own class all day long so I don't have a lot to do with the older children but the young ones talk about their older brothers and sisters a lot.

In my opinion there is too much tolerance at home; I understand that it is no longer allowed to hit a child but parents don't even find other ways to punish their children. I had a mother complain to me the other day that she could not control her six-year old. I ask you, six years old; what will she do when he is sixteen? I told her he needed more sleep, that he was always tired in class and all she could reply was that he liked to watch the television in his bedroom.

This particular mother does not work but a lot of the mothers do go to work and they use the television as a way of getting some peace; they park the children in front of it so that they can relax. Even the type of games children play has changed; they no longer go out and play with their friends, preferring their computers or Playstations.

Also a lot of children spend a great deal of time with their grandmother or with a nanny and of course they don't receive the same discipline that they would from their parents. I know there are parents who set clear parameters for their children, restricting the time they can watch television or play computer games, but they are fewer than before.'

'What about the curriculum?' I asked. 'Have you seen many changes?'

'Not really. They have renamed certain subjects, Nature Study for example is now Environmental Studies, but basically they are much the same. With the little ones I teach them about plants, parts of the body or animals. We do art, music, religion and stories in the afternoons and numbers, reading and writing in the mornings. I enjoy the music classes; we do rhythm, melody and dance. Of course with the little ones we do a lot of improvisation, using all sorts of things as musical instruments: old bottles, spoons, shells, sticks. I belong to the *Musica Tradicional de la Danza*, a group of teachers that meet once a month to share their ideas and their work. We design new choreography and practice it together before we try it out on the children. It's great fun. The only time I don't have my class is when they go for English. The new law has made it obligatory for the children to learn English from six years old, which is good because they can absorb the language much easier.'

'Is religion still obligatory?' I asked her.

'Well that's not very clear; it's still on the timetable but it doesn't count towards the end of year results. The policy is a bit vague; if the child is not Catholic then they can be excused from the lesson. I have four children that this applies to; but what can I do with them? They are too small to work alone and there's no other teacher to look after them. I talked to their parents and they said to include them in the lessons on religion because at least then they would be working.'

'What about after school?' I asked.

'The children have a long day, especially if they come by bus, or their mother is working. We start at nine and finish at six in the evening, with a two and a half hour lunch break, then for those that want to stay there are various activities: basketball, gymnastics, football, handball, music. These are all voluntary and the parents have to pay for them. At midday children can stay for lunch if they wish and take part in some activity afterwards, but there are no teachers on duty, only monitors.

When the school was private the parents paid for everything, now they just have to pay for the bus, lunches and extra-curricular activities. Many public schools are much better equipped than the private ones, especially when it comes to computer technology and sports facilities. My own school does not have a lot of money for re-investment because it is owned by share-holders and of course they want their dividends.

There's a lot of politics in education; originally children were expected to learn to read as soon as possible. Then when LOGSE was introduced we were told that children must not be taught to read before they were six years old. Now it is changing back again.'

'So what is your opinion?'

'I think children should learn to read as soon as they can, while their minds are at their most receptive. Some children attend pre-school nurseries and when they arrive here they can sound out the letters and even read a bit. It is so important for them to read. Every morning after I have talked to them for a bit we start on the reading; I have one on the left side of my desk and another one on the right and I make sure I hear everyone in my class every day. We are not allowed, by law, to set the children any homework but I disregard that; I send them home with their reading books and the page they have to read each night clearly marked. At the beginning of each new school year I call a parents' meeting and I explain to them that I will be sending work home when it is necessary. Last year I had twenty-eight children in my class and only four could read when they arrived; by the end of the year they could all read.

Sometimes I have a child with learning difficulties and I get the child psychologist to assess them so that they can have extra help, but the parents don't always like it. I think some of them feel that I am saying that their child is of a lower standing or something. But of course once I know what the child's problems are then there are lots of special exercises I can do with them to help.

Another change in my job is the amount of paperwork I have to do now that we have a new law on education, LOE. All the children's records are to be computerized. We have a new computer program called SENECA and have to input both personal and academic data. I'm not sure how it will work out because I haven't had to use the system yet.'

'What about your personal life?'

'Well my husband works in a bank and as you know I have one son; he's twenty-four and he lives at home.'

Her son had just come in and was in the garden talking to his grandfather.

'I would have liked to have three or four children but as I was working I decided against it; I wasn't happy leaving my son with a nanny,' she continued. 'When he was born I had three months off then I went back to work. At first I had a girl living in to look after him, but she almost killed him by giving him yogurt with salt instead of sugar, so we got rid of her. I sent him to a nursery for a few years then he came to school with me. I could have sent him to a different school but in the end it was easier for him to come with me.

It's a long day during term time; I always used to come home at lunch-time to prepare the meal and then of course had to go back to work again. Nowadays we eat at a local restaurant during the week; they have a very good set meal for seven euros. It is much easier for me. My husband does very little to help me in the home; he has a traditional mentality when it comes to the role of husbands.

Despite the fact that I have two months holiday in the summer I get very tired these days; I would like to retire but I won't be able to until I am at least sixty-one. I would also like to take an English course because although I studied it when I was at college I have forgotten a lot. It would be nice to take a month's trip to England and do an intensive course but I can't leave my parents. We always come to stay in this summer house with them so that I can look after them. They are getting old now and I don't like my father to drive, so I drive, I do the shopping, take my mother to Mass and generally look after them. I couldn't leave them for a month. They are alright when they are living in their flat in Málaga because they have everything to hand and anyway my aunt, who is much younger, lives with them, but here it is much more difficult for them. My mother goes to Mass every evening when she is in Málaga because she can easily walk to the church.

I don't mind looking after my parents; I'm glad they are both so well and happy. I would never want to see either of them living in a home, not whilst I was able to care for them. I know that sometimes you have no option; my friend's mother has Alzheimers and she has had to put her in a residential home because she could not cope. It is very sad. I don't know what I would do if we had to face that decision but there are lots of options: I could get someone to live in for example.'

'What about hobbies? Do you have time for any hobbies?' I asked her.

'I have a passion for genealogy,' she replied, jumping up and getting some folders from the desk. 'I have been tracing our family names: Hermosa and Bueno. I have traced the Bueno side of the family back to the fifteenth century.'

She opened the folders and showed me her research, beautifully laid out in a cursive script with both illustrations and photographs.

'I've been working on it for six years and now I'm not sure if I can get any further.'

Education

In 1923 when General Primo de Rivera came to power he curtailed academic freedom in Spanish higher education causing many professors and intellectuals to go into exile.

The Second Republic reinstated the academic freedom of the universities, removed the influence of the church from the curriculum and introduced free primary education for everyone. These changes however were short-lived and Franco soon imposed his own strictly Catholic and Nationalist views on the education system. In 1936 a statue of the Virgin Mary was placed in all schools and children were instructed to pray daily for the successful conclusion of the war.

While he was in power education was for the elite; it was highly centralised and strictly controlled both politically and administratively. The Church had the right to intervene in a curriculum that was biased in favour of religion, Franco and the State. Catholic religious instruction was mandatory in all schools and the Church was given the right to establish its own universities. Government spending on education was well below the European average and only 70% of fourteen year olds were in school. The highest rate of illiteracy was amongst women in rural areas.

Girls particularly suffered from the new regime; wartime legislation stated that girls' education should be "separate, subordinate and domestic". From as early as 1936 Franco decreed that there be no co-educational schools and if necessary the boys would attend in the mornings and the girls in the afternoons. He also stipulated that only women should teach in girls' schools, which given the lack of educated women teachers meant that the girls did not receive the same level of academic education as the boys. Women teachers were instructed to prepare their pupils for their important future function in the home, teaching them sewing, cooking, gardening and household skills.

In 1970 the General Law on Education attempted to reorganise the entire Spanish education system but it was ineffective and what reforms were enacted soon became out of date.

Since Franco's death the government has decentralised much of the responsibility for education to the seventeen regional autonomous communities into which Spain is now divided, through a series of Acts:

1983 University Reform Law
1985 the Right to Education Law (LODE)
1990 the Law on the General Organisation of the Educational System (LOGSE)
1995 the Organic Law Regulating the Participation, Evaluation and Governance of Schools (LOPEGCE)
2006 the Organic Law of Education (LOE)

To ensure that there was continuity and homogeneity within the regions the Ministry of Education established minimum academic requirements for 65% of the curriculum, leaving the remainder to reflect regional priorities. By 1986 national spending on education was on par with the rest of Europe and the process of decentralisation was under way.

The administration of the education system looks like this:
Ministry of Education and Science
State School Council
National Advisory Body

Conference of Education Counsellors (Minister of Education and the chief Education Officers from each Autonomous Region meet at least once a year.)

Education Councils (one in each of the Autonomous Regions)

Local School Councils (Elect the School Principal and are made up of the School Principal, chief of academic studies, local government representative, teachers and students. They have an administrative and supervisory role.)

School Principal (implements the decisions of the School Council)

By 1995 compulsory schooling had been extended to sixteen years of age and the number of public schools had increased from 1,100 in 1975 to 3,000. Nowadays children can attend pre-school from the ages of three to six; when they are six years-old they must attend primary school until the age of twelve then secondary education until they reach sixteen. If they wish, children can continue to study for their Bachillerato until they are eighteen years old, when they can either leave school and go to work or move on to higher education. Literacy rates are now 98% for both men and women.

PILAR born in Caceres in 1957

Pilar is married and has one daughter. She was born in Caceres in Extremadura and now lives in Cádiz where she works as a teacher.

I found myself sitting next to Pilar one day at lunch. She was a well built woman with big, sad eyes. The conversation turned to Franco and the past:

'I remember my grandmother telling me how hard things were during the war and afterwards. If you lived in the country there was usually something to eat: chickens or vegetables, but if you lived in a city there was nothing. Madrid was the worst. There was nothing but bread; people lived on bread.

My grandmother's neighbour's husband was a Red and was hiding from the *Guardia Civil* in the *sierra*, the mountains behind the city. One weekend he came down to visit his wife and children. Another neighbour saw him and immediately contacted the police who went straight to his house and shot him through the head in front of his family. No arrest, no trial. There was a lot of that then; if anyone had a grudge against someone they would denounce them to the *Guardia Civil*.

Things were not much better after the war had finished. My father died of a heart attack when he was only forty and my mother was left to bring up ten children. She had no money and little food; it was a very hard life.

I went to a public school and because I was clever and studied hard I did very well; I had very good reports and I was able to qualify for one of the grants that they gave to workers' children so that I could go to college to study Business Studies. It was not a very big college; in our class there were about eight boys and fourteen girls. The girls were allowed to study alongside the boys but during the breaks we were kept separate. One day, when I was eighteen years old, a boy in my class offered me a lift home in his car. We were just leaving the car-park when an armed policeman stopped us and pointed his gun into the car and told me to get out. He said I was not allowed to leave the college in the company of a boy. I tried to protest but he just kept waving his gun at me so in the end I got out and went to wait for the bus.

One of our subjects was Civil Law and I still have the text book we used. I wanted to keep it so that I could show my daughter the page where it said that it was against the law for any woman to sign a document. I think my daughter and maybe my grandchildren will find it interesting.

I live in Cádiz now. My husband, who is a civil servant, was moved here with his job and so I asked for a transfer. I remember that we used to go to the cinema a lot, but I wouldn't go in until the *Nodos* had finished.'

When she saw my blank look she explained:

'Before every film they used to show a newsreel film of Franco and what he had been doing during the past week: fishing, going to Mass, all sorts of things. These were always referred to as the *Nodos*. I hated them. I hated Franco. There was never any news of the outside world; nobody knew what was happening outside Spain; nobody even knew what was happening inside Spain. No-one ever travelled. It was all very confined.

Nowadays people know more about the world. My own daughter for example, has travelled all over Europe. She's twenty-three now and she's already been to Boston and London to study English and this year she's going to Dublin.'

Biblioteca Popular Francesca Bonnemaison

This public library in Barcelona was founded in 1909 by a group of women for the use of working women. It is considered to be the oldest women's library in the world and was founded with the idea of educating women to be better wives and daughters. It aimed to improve cultural awareness and raise the level of women's education. Its original name was the Institut de Cultura i Biblioteca Popular de la Doña, and included a school for teaching professional skills. Besides having a wide range of fiction the library contained an eclectic selection of books including cookery books, fashion magazines and books on physical education.

The library opened with just over six hundred books. When Franco came to power the library was cleansed of many of its books: those in Catalan and anything opposed to Franco. However unlike books confiscated from other libraries these were not destroyed but stored in a depository until after the death of Franco when they were reinstated. Today the library has 46,000 volumes, including many works written by and for women.

In 1976 the library took on its present name, being called after one of its original founders, Francesca Bonnemaison. Francesca herself was not a working woman, nor was she a feminist; she was a housewife who liked to do charity work and she held strong beliefs about the role of women, believing that a woman's place was at home with her family. She used the library and the school to promote her ideas. When the Civil War began Francesca went into exile and gave the library building to the city on the condition that it should always remain a women's library.

For thirty years after the war the school and the library were used by the women's section of the Falange party.

MARIA DE LOS DOLORES ANGELES JUANA born in Melilla 1941

Maria Dolores (Lolina) is married with 4 children. She was born in Melilla. She spoke mostly about her mother **Dolores** who was born in Morocco in 1915 and worked as a teacher and broadcaster. Her mother was married to an officer in the Nationalist army and was left a widow with five young children to bring up on her own.

My friend leant across and whispered in my ear:

'You should interview Lolina; her mother had a very interesting life.'

She nodded towards an elderly woman sitting across the lunch table. We had just finished playing a Christmas game of golf and were about to tuck into a typical Spanish lunch.

A few weeks later I was sitting in a corner of the same restaurant with Lolina, my voice recorder in front of me, two large coffees on the table and an ample supply of Lolina's favourite cigarettes. Her mother had died only a few months previously, aged ninety two, but she was happy to tell me what she could remember of her mother's life:

DOLORES 1915-2007

'My mother was Spanish but she was born in Morocco. Not long after they were married her parents moved from Berja in Almeria because my grandfather had lost his job and needed work and went to live in North Africa. He managed to get a job as station master in Zeluan in Morocco. In those days the railway was very important to the economy of the region and of Spain; it linked Melilla on the coast with the coal mines in the Eastern Rif. Although my grandfather was based in

Zeluan he took a house in Melilla for his wife and children. This meant that my mother only saw him at the weekends because he was responsible for all the stations on the line and spent the whole week travelling between them.

This was the time of the Moroccan wars and the country had been split between the French and Spanish colonialists. In the war of 1914 my grandfather was captured and imprisoned; he might very well have died there if it hadn't been for a Moorish soldier who recognised him. My grandmother had always given water and food to this man whenever he passed by their house and he saw the chance to return the favour. He removed his cloak and gave it to my grandfather, telling him to put it on and hide himself among the goats that had been loaded into the goods wagon of a train that was just about to leave. My grandfather settled down amongst the goats and escaped; without a doubt that man saved his life.

My mother's family, unlike my father's, was of humble origins; there was always enough to eat but they were not rich. My grandmother was a very generous and religious woman and would always give to those in need. I remember my mother telling me that one day she went with her to buy some new sheets and on the way to the shops they met a woman she knew. The woman was crying and said she had no money to pay her bills and they were going to cut off her electricity. My grandmother gave her the money she had saved for the sheets; she told her that her need was greater than hers and that she could buy new sheets another time. That was very typical of her. There were always people coming to her house and no matter how little she had she would find some food to give them. According to my mother it was not just that she gave them things but she did it in a subtle way, so that they were not embarrassed to take them.

My grandmother never worked; her life was spent looking after the family and raising her children. She had five children: four daughters and a son. Only my mother was born in Morocco, the others were all born in Melilla, but they all had Spanish nationality. My grandmother brought her children up to respect other people, whatever their origins. She was a very intelligent woman and she wanted all her children to be educated alike. My grandfather however did not approve of educating his daughters; he said that a girl's place was in the home. My mother and her sisters went to school but he did not want them to have anything more than the basic education that was usually given to girls. What he didn't realise was that while he was away working my mother spent every night studying for her Baccalaureate. It took her seven years; she had no text books of her own so she shared those of a neighbour that lived in the flat above. He would lower them down to her in a basket every evening so that she could study and then haul them back up in the morning so that he could take them to school. She had no money to buy notebooks and paper so she would use whatever she could find, even the backs of the cinema flyers that they used to distribute in the street and bits of wrapping paper that she carefully removed from the shopping and pressed flat. She worked all night, every night, writing by candlelight. After seven years she passed her Baccalaureate and was awarded a grant to study architecture in Madrid. It had always been her great dream to be the first woman architect in Spain. Of course by then they could not keep her studies hidden from my grandfather any longer; she and my grandmother had to confess what had been happening all those years. My grandfather was very surprised but not angry; nevertheless he refused point blank to allow her to go to Madrid to study. He said that the only suitable jobs for women were as a nurse or a teacher. If she wanted to work he would allow her to study to become a teacher in Melilla, but there was no way he would allow an unmarried daughter of his to go to Madrid to study.

So my mother became a teacher in a school in Melilla but she didn't just teach, she also made radio broadcasts for children, telling stories, reciting poems and or just talking about things that might interest them; she wrote articles on social matters for the local newspaper and for a short time she was a photographic model advertising some product, but I can't remember what it was, toothpaste I think. She was a very religious young woman and besides attending church regularly she used to help the nuns that worked in the Red Cross Hospital in Melilla.

Melilla at that time was a garrison town; there were over four hundred thousand soldiers stationed there. She told me that they used to say that there were at least seven men for every available woman. It was while she was writing a piece for the newspaper about one of the local dances that she met my father; he asked her to dance the *pasodoble* with him and that was the start of their relationship.

My father was twenty years older than her. He had lived the life of a single army captain, sharing his apartment with other officers and having numerous girlfriends. Now he had decided it was time to settle down. He wrote to my grandfather explaining that his intentions regarding my mother were serious and that although he currently had a debt of three thousand pesetas, he planned to pay it off before becoming engaged to her. Even in those days it was an unusual relationship because of the difference in their ages, so he wanted to reassure my grandfather that he was an honourable man. I think my father was attracted by my mother's intelligence and the purity of her life, very unlike the other women he had known. On my mother's part, it was the first and only love of her life.

On 17th July 1936 the Civil War started. My father was ordered to go with his soldiers to Spain, to Cordoba and the front line. There was a shortage of boats to take the soldiers across the Straits of Gibraltar and he and his men were transported in a boat provided by the mayor of Melilla. Once he was in Cordoba, in the Nationalist zone, he began to feel very lonely; most of the other men had their wives with them. He decided to ask my mother to travel to Cordoba to marry him but my grandfather refused to allow it. As far as he was concerned it was not right for an unmarried woman to visit her fiancé, even if the intention was to get married. If her fiancé couldn't come to Melilla then they would have to get married by proxy. A friend and colleague of my father's stood in as the proxy groom and the wedding took place in Melilla in March 1937; only then would my grandfather allow my mother to travel to Cordoba to be with her husband. When she arrived she was not able to see him straight away because he was at the front, fighting; she had to stay in a women's hostel for almost a month before they could be together. They stayed in Cordoba for a few years and the first of their children was born there in December 1938.

After a few years my father was moved back to Melilla, where I was born and then he was transferred to Castellon, north of Madrid where the rest of my brothers and sisters were born. He had a job as a military adviser to a minister, but he never had a lot of money because although my father had received many military decorations for the service he had given to Franco, his pay was never very great.'

At this point Lolina stopped and showed me a photograph of her mother and father. It was a studio photograph of a handsome couple, he in his army uniform and cap, with three rows of medals pinned to his chest and her with her hair caught up under a black lace mantilla looking like a thirties film star.

'He had more medals than that,' she said pointing to the photograph. Then she continued:

'My father's family came from a different social strata to my mother's; they were very upper class. I remember my mother being astounded the first time she ate at her mother-in-law's house; they had seven courses of food and their servants not only ate in a different room, usually the kitchen, but they ate different food. In my mother's house everyone sat down together to eat. I remember that when I was a child I was often in trouble with my grandmother and was made to eat my meal in the bathroom because I had broken some protocol of the dining table. For instance nobody was allowed to finish their meal before my grandparents had finished.

Despite the fact that they had little money I think they had a very happy life and my mother never complained; she always believed in Divine Providence and taught her children to do the same. She said God would provide and he did. When they moved to Castellon, she asked for a transfer to a teaching post there. My father did not mind her working; she had a housemaid and her young sister to help her in the home so everything ran smoothly. Her sister had come from Melilla to live with them soon after they arrived in Castellon and she stayed with my mother all her life; she never married.

After my parents had been married for eighteen years my father died of lung cancer, leaving a very young widow with five children between the ages of six and sixteen to care for, and very little money with which to do it. Her widow's pension from the army was barely enough to live on, only nine hundred pesetas a month, so she had no option but to continue working as a teacher. Before he died my father had made her promise that all the children, even the girls, would have a good education, but after a few months she realised that the only way to guarantee this was to send her children to boarding schools run and paid for by the army. My elder sister went to Salamanca and the rest of us went to schools in Madrid. This was a tremendous sacrifice for my mother because she had to stay in Castellon without her children and I know she missed us terribly, although she was always very busy.

Soon after my father died my mother began working with the nuns of the *Obreras de la Cruz*, a religious order that helped the sick; she would visit hospitals, caring for sick patients, sew clothes for the poor, help the nuns with their quarterly magazine, whatever was required of her. She was the first lay person to join the organisation; nowadays they have many lay volunteers, but my mother was the first.

Our youngest brother was only eight when he was sent away to school and one Easter when my mother went to visit him, he complained bitterly that he missed her and that all his friends saw their mothers every weekend. My mother was very upset by this outburst so decided to do something about it. At that time they were building some new flats near his school so, despite the fact that she had hardly any money, she paid a small deposit, a thousand pesetas, I think, to reserve one. Then she went back to Castellon and handed in her notice to the head teacher, saying that she would not be returning after the summer holidays because she was going to live in Madrid. She asked him to arrange a transfer for her. She bought herself a ticket in the national lottery and prayed to God every day that he would let her win just enough money to buy the flat; she did not want to win a single peseta more. After a couple of months she had heard nothing about her transfer, so she went to see the head master. He had not sent off her request for a transfer; like everybody else he thought she was mad. She insisted he do it right away and she told her landlord that she would not need the flat in Castellon anymore and continued to pray that she would win the lottery. And she did win. She won more money than she needed so she paid the balance for her flat and gave the rest to one of her sisters.

My mother got a new job as a teacher in an Army school in Madrid and joined the Madrid branch of the *Obreras de la Cruz* so that she could continue with her voluntary work, which now included not only helping in the hospitals but also teaching gypsy children to read and write. She also helped in her local parish, visiting sick people and looking after the poor. Her life was always full; she listened to the radio and read the newspaper every day so that she could keep up with what was happening in the country. To earn some extra money she sometimes had American students staying in the flat whilst we were away at school. She was a very sociable person and every Sunday afternoon she invited her friends to afternoon tea with her. She was also very pious; she went to Mass regularly and visited the church every day. Every Christmas she continued to buy lottery tickets for herself and her friends; I think they all thought she would be lucky again, so liked her to buy the tickets for them, but although she won small amounts she never again won the big prize.

Anyway that's how we all came to live in Madrid: us five children, my mother, one of her sisters and her brother-in-law.'

'Brother-in-law?' I asked.

'Yes, my mother had a sister, Africa, who had stayed in Melilla in the family home; she had not married until she was fifty-five. Her fiancé, Fernando did not want to marry because he knew that he was going blind and said he did not want to become a burden to her, so they remained engaged for thirty years. I think he was just so well looked after at home that he did not want to leave. However once his mother and his sister had died and he was left alone, he changed his mind and decided to marry my aunt, who was still crazy about him. The house, where she lived in Melilla was very old and in a bad state of repair, so they sold it and bought a flat in Madrid near my mother. Some years later when my aunt Africa died, Fernando, who by now was blind, moved in with my mother. She looked after him until she was no longer able to look after herself.

She continued to live there in that same flat in Madrid until she became too old to manage on her own and then she, her sister and Fernando came to Málaga. My mother and my aunt came to live with me and Fernando went to live in a residential home close by. We really did everything for my mother to make her feel at home but she was not happy in Málaga. We even organised for the priest to come once a week to give her Holy Communion. She had always been so independent and now she was eighty-four and she could not walk nor take care of herself. She hardly ever spoke to anyone and never asked for anything, just answered me with a "yes" or a "no"; I think she was unhappy that she was no longer in control of her own life. My aunt died first; she had been suffering from Altzeimers for some years and then my mother died aged ninety-two.'

The Catholic Church and women's rights

If you visit some of the churches in Spain you may come across "las celdas de las emparedadas", the cells of recluses or literally of "walled-up women". In Astorga in León in northern Spain the chapel of San Esteban is built alongside the 14th century Catholic church of Santa Maria. In the chapel there is a tiny, narrow cell with yellow stone walls, a dirt floor and one high, small window with iron bars. This is the "celda de las emparedadas" where women were imprisoned as a punishment for sexual crimes. The woman was placed inside and the entrance blocked by large stones. If the people of the town had any compassion for the woman they fed her through the small window; if not she died. Above the tiny window is carved this warning: "Remember my judgement because yours will be the same. As for me yesterday, so for you today."

Not all the women walled up in this way were being punished. Some entered the cells voluntarily so that they could live a life dedicated to prayer and penance. These recluses remained in their tiny cells until the day they died at which point the cells were completely walled up and became their tombs. Although in theory women were free to come and go, in practice they were restricted to their homes or the cloister; they were expected to be wives and mothers or nuns.

During the rule of Franco the Catholic Church exerted a great deal of power over women, the family and education. Franco came from a strong religious background and when he took power he turned to the church to help him regulate and control society. There was to be no freedom of religious choice whilst he was in power. The Catholic Church was in turn a fervent supporter of the dictator and his social programme.

Women were exhorted to lead good Christian lives, to look to their duties as mothers, wives and members of the parish. They were encouraged to go to mass regularly and spend their time raising children and doing charitable works. If they did not want to do this there were two other options open to them: if they had a true spiritual calling they could devote their lives to prayer and contemplation within a convent or they could become "beatas", lay holy women who lived a life of prayer and charity outside of both marriage and the convent.

Today Spain is still considered a Catholic country but only 14% of its young people say they are religious and the number of priests and monks entering the seminaries is shrinking. Religious holy days are still celebrated as national holidays and the Spanish like to marry in church and have their children take their First Communion but for many it is devoid of any religious meaning. General church attendance has fallen. A survey in 2007 stated that although over seventy percent of Spaniards claimed to be Catholics, only thirty-six percent were practising. More women than men attend church; forty-five percent of those women interviewed said they went to mass regularly.

Since Franco's death and the rise of democracy the Church has had an ongoing battle with the government over such issues as abortion, divorce, gay marriage and contraception. In January 2009 a primary school in Valladolid was ordered to remove the crucifixes from their classroom walls because they violated the "non-confessional" approach of modern society.

According to the director of religious affairs in the Justice Ministry Spain is neither Catholic theoretically, culturally or politically. He said that Spain was now a multicultural society and as such should revise its definition of religious liberty so that all religions are judged equal.

LUI was born in Málaga in 1947

Lui was born in Málaga but as a child lived in most of the big towns in Spain because of her father's job. She has been married twice, has one son from her first marriage and two adopted children. She lived for many years in Madrid and now splits her time between Málaga and El Rocio. She has never had paid employment but does a lot of charity work.

I arrived early and a slightly harassed Lui opened the door.

'Come in, but please excuse me for a moment, I haven't finished putting my make-up on. Take a seat and I'll be right back.'

I walked through to the room she had indicated with a wave of her ringed hand and sat on the sofa, overlooking the garden. This was the television room, a cosy room off the main lounge. Lui's house was large and well furnished in typical Spanish middle-class splendour with lots of dark, polished wood, glass surfaces and ornaments. The walls were covered with paintings, many of which I later discovered were done by her; they looked very professional. As I waited I was aware of a domestic help working in the background. After a few minutes Lui returned, immaculately groomed. She was still a beautiful woman despite her years.

'Sorry to keep you waiting,' she said.

I knew Lui from the golf club; she was the organiser of a major golf competition that raised money for the charity *Manos Unidas*, (Hands United), each year. I asked her how she had got started.

'Well it was really by accident,' she replied. 'The wife of my jeweller is very involved with the charity *Manos Unidas* and she was looking for someone to organise a golf competition to raise money. One day when her husband came to see me about some new jewellery, she came with him. She asked me if I would like to organise something. I was very unsure about taking it on; it was a lot of responsibility and I don't like to do things unless I can do them well. Anyway she convinced me that I should try and in fact it turned out to be a great success. We raised thousands of euros to help build a school and improve water supplies.

I am running another competition for them this year but I think I will change the format. As it is a charity that raises money for children I think it would be nice if it was a "Parents and Children" competition; you know dad playing with his son or mum with her daughter, any combination really.'

'Are you a very religious person?' I asked, remembering the shrine to the Virgin in the hall as I had come in and looking at the painting of the Virgin on the wall.

'I suppose so,' she replied. 'I'm Catholic as are all my family and I'm very much attached to the Virgin of Rocio. The people of Andalucia are very fond of the Virgin Mary, and I am particularly fond of the Virgin of Rocio. I don't know what it is about her but, when you go in and see her and you hear of the miracles that she has performed, you become caught in her spell. We are members of the brotherhood in Madrid; there are one hundred and three brotherhoods of Rocio. Each May for the last thirty years we have made the pilgrimage to the town of Rocio to see her.'

She explained that the Virgin of Rocio was in a chapel in Rocio, a village on the edge of the Doñana National Park in Huelva, a wildlife area of marshes, sand dunes and woodland. As legend has it, King Alfonso X had the chapel built after the reconquest of the area in 1262 and a statue of the Virgin Mary installed inside. Today it is the focus of a national pilgrimage and more than a million people congregate in Rocio each year to celebrate the day of the Virgin.

'We don't walk all the way, just the first part, as far as the church then join up with the rest of our brotherhood and travel by car. Lots of people go on horseback or in gypsy caravans, walking part of the way and sleeping rough. I don't like sleeping with all those people so for the first few years we towed a caravan and slept in that then some friends of ours, the founders of our brotherhood, invited us to stay in their house. We did that each year for about twenty years until a few years ago when we bought our own house in the centre of Rocio. It is a very old house and very damp because it is built on sand; the whole town is on sand and the streets are unpaved. We have done a lot of work to the house but we need to do more to get rid of the damp, like build proper foundations. I love it there and I love the pilgrimage. All the women wear flamenco dresses, and boots because of the sand, and the men wear typical Andalusian costume; it is very colourful with all the horses and ox-carts and caravans.'

She paused for a moment to answer her mobile telephone; it was for her domestic help, Luba, a young Czech woman.

'Let me tell you about *Semana Santa*,' she said when she returned. 'I don't really have a strong attachment to the processions of *Semana Santa* because I lived for much of my life away from Málaga, but when I was a child, each year, on Palm Sunday, I used to walk with the other children in the procession, carrying a palm leaf. One year when I went to collect my clothes the priest said that I was too old to take part anymore; I was ten. In those days women and girls didn't take part in the Easter processions, the only exception had been the Palm Sunday one. I was so upset at this news I went rushing straight to another church to see if they would let me take part in something. At first the priest said no, but then he relented and said that if I cut my hair off, wore boy's shoes and didn't speak I could take part in the procession just that once. I did and I wore a long cloak and a tall, pointed hood, so nobody knew I was a girl.

Nowadays of course women can take part in all the processions if they wish; they sometimes even carry the throne with the Virgin.'

'Tell me about your family,' I said next.

'Oh, Joan, if I told you everything about my family you could write a book just on them. Well there's my mother; she lives upstairs. She's eighty-three now and four years ago she had a stroke so I brought her here to live with me. She recovered quite well from the stroke but then she fell and broke her hip, so she hardly ever leaves her room. But she has everything there in her room and she has Luba to help her when I'm not here.

When my mother was young she worked in the Ladies' section of the *Falange* movement with a group of friends; they taught young girls how to sew, embroider and dance. She was very athletic as a young woman and played basketball. She and my father met in Málaga, got married and had me. I was the only child because my mother was not able to have any more. When she was pregnant with me she developed preeclampsia, a blood disorder and was very ill. At one point my father was told he had to choose between his wife and his child. Luckily we both survived and I was born premature, at seven months.

Although I was born in Málaga I have lived most of my life in other towns because of my father's job. He had a fantastic job, setting up the installations for radio and television broadcasting stations throughout Andalusia. In the fifties and sixties there was no television and little radio in Spain, so we moved from city to city with his job. We lived in Cordoba, Seville, all over Andalusia. Of course that meant new schools for me each time but I didn't mind; I was very adaptable and they were always very good schools, and always convents. On one occasion they sent me to a boarding school because they thought it would be less disruptive for my studies, but I couldn't stand being away from my mother, so they brought me home again. I think all the travelling gave me an advantage because in those days nobody travelled anywhere. Also we were very well-off because my father earned a lot of money; at a time when salaries were between eight and ten thousand pesetas a year he was earning three thousand pesetas a month because of the commissions he received on each new installation.

I met my husband in Málaga when we were here on holiday one summer; I was sixteen and I was sunbathing on the beach with my friends. We fell in love and when I was twenty we got married. Our son, José was born the following year. Then two years later my husband died of kidney failure; he was only thirty. So at twenty-three I was left a widow with a two year old son. I was heartbroken. I had to leave Málaga; I was wandering around crying all the time, like one of those women that follow the thrones in the *Semana Santa* processions, dressed in black and constantly weeping. It was time to start a new stage in my life, so I moved to Madrid with my parents and my son. My father was about to retire anyway and he fancied moving back to his home town of Toledo, on the outskirts of Madrid. I look back on those years and realise I was just a child then; at the time I felt very mature, especially because I had travelled so much, but I was really very young.

Well while I was in Madrid I met my present husband, Rafa. He was the cousin of a friend of mine. It was love at first sight. I used to go everywhere with my son and Rafa was wonderful with him, taking him to the park and to watch the aeroplanes. Sadly when we got married we found out that Rafa couldn't have any children.'

I looked at her in surprise because I knew that there were two other children in the family.

'Rafa and Rocio are adopted,' she explained. '*Que cosa!* I never planned to adopt any children but just look what happened. I tell you my story would fill a book.

One day I was listening to the radio when I heard this famous broadcaster talking about "The message of peace"; it was a charity that helped abandoned children. As I listened I thought I could help with that so I took down the telephone number and rang them. I said I would be willing to help and they promised to get in touch. Well I thought they would want me to serve meals or help at a centre or something, so I wasn't prepared when after a couple of months they rang and asked me to go and see a child who had been left with his grandparents. His mother was in hospital suffering from TB and they didn't know where his father was. I hesitated for a moment until they told me his name was Rafa; just fancy, what a coincidence. Well of course I had to go and see him.'

She laughed and added:

'My friends always called me Augustina de Aragón because I would jump straight into any situation, fearless. And that's what I did; I went straight there to see this boy. My husband said it wasn't a good idea to get involved in someone else's problems but I wouldn't listen to him, I just kept thinking about this poor little boy, with no-one to look after him.

They took me to see him at his grandparents' house. Well what a sight. The house was awful, small and dirty and it stunk of pee. There was a line of unwashed nappies hung up to dry in the kitchen and everything was filthy. *En el nombre del padre,* I tell you, it was dreadful. The boy was sitting in the corner; he was skin and bone, dressed in rags and so dirty. The grandmother was old and bent, dressed completely in black; as she shuffled towards me I thought she was a witch. The grandfather was an ugly old man, with a fierce scowl that frightened me. In another corner of the room sat a second man, who seemed to be mentally retarded. I tell you, it was awful. The grandparents were desperate to get rid of the boy; they wanted me to take him right away but I said I would have to speak to the mother first.

I visited the mother in hospital and she begged me to take him just until she came out of hospital. I didn't know what to do. What could I do with such a sick child at home? In the end I felt I had no choice, I couldn't leave him there; so I went back to the grandparents and collected the boy.

Anyway the first thing I did was take him to the doctor. The doctor took one look at him and said:

"What have you brought me here, girl?"

The boy was three years old and weighed only eight kilos. The doctor examined him and said he had very advanced TB, he was covered in vermin and seriously underdeveloped both physically and mentally. I just didn't know what to do; I felt obliged to look after him even though I did not want him in the house with my own son. I had no alternative but it was a struggle with him from the first moment. Even his teeth were a problem; his baby teeth did not fall out naturally; they all had to be extracted. I tell you it scared me to look in his mouth and see a double set of teeth.

Well after a few months I had to go away on a trip to Brazil, so I went to see his mother and explained that I would leave him with someone to care for him while I was away and that when I came back we would have to talk about his future. You wouldn't believe how bad things had become at home with such a small child; I just can't explain to you how awful it was. His mother said she would soon be able to look after him herself, but when I returned to Madrid after my trip she had left the hospital and nobody could trace her. She had disappeared. The grandparents refused to have their grandson back and by then I could understand why they did not want him; he was a monster. So I had no alternative but to keep him and that was when we decided it was best to adopt him.

Well Rafa is in his thirties now and I can tell you he has brought me and my family nothing but suffering and unhappiness in all those years. He was thrown out of every school we sent him to; one school even expelled him twice. He became a drug addict and do you know where he is now? In prison for kidnapping a small child.'

She shook her head in desperation.

'He's a psychopath. Look up the definition of psychopath and he is everything that it says: unable to accept responsibility for his actions, callous, irresponsible, delinquent, pathological liar, manipulative and more. That's what I have brought up. When he was only twelve years old a psychiatrist told me he was already pre-psychopathic. He was in his own world; he had no friends and no interest in anything. We never gave him a birthday party; he had no-one to invite. He never laughed; he never talked; no-one ever telephoned him. He would sit for hours on end crashing two toys together or just staring at the floor. He was never aggressive but he used to say that he could hear voices inside his head. Some people say he is mad, but he's not mad, he's a psychopath and there is no cure for that.

When he was eighteen he went into the army. I thought thank God, I'll have a year of peace, but they threw him out after only two days. From the army! He would sleep on the beach and not come home for eight or nine days and we never knew where he was. Life was impossible.'

'It's strange that you risked adopting a second child after such a bad experience,' I commented.

'Just so. It's odd, isn't it. But I believe in destiny. I didn't go looking for either child; God sent them to me. I had my own son, my fantastic husband, my home and a full life. I wasn't looking for anything more, but God thought differently.

We had just started the adoption process for Rafa when I had a telephone call from a woman asking me if I wanted to adopt her baby who was due to be born soon. I told her I was already going through the process for another child and asked her how she had got my telephone number. It turned out that this woman was from a good family and when she had become pregnant her father had told her to get rid of the baby; she wouldn't abort it so she tried to find someone to adopt it. She had been to see the same woman, Carmen, who was organising the adoption of Rafa and had seen our name on some papers on her desk. Then I remembered that a friend of mine was considering adopting a baby, so I said I would tell her about it and in the meantime I suggested that the woman should come to the house to see us.

When I put the telephone down I suddenly realised what the date was: it was 7th October, the anniversary of the death of my first husband and the day of the Virgin de Rosario. I suddenly felt that this child had been sent for me; it was a present for me. My husband did not agree with me; he said it wasn't a good idea, that we had enough problems with the other child, but in the end he said it was up to me.

Well, when the mother arrived to see us, she was a beautiful, elegant young woman.'

She broke off her narrative and asked me:

'Do you know my daughter? This is her.'

She handed me a photograph of a beautiful, dark haired young woman.

'Well her mother looked just like her. She had no way of caring for the baby without her parents help so she wanted to be sure it went to a good home. We talked for a bit, then when she said she thought the baby was a girl that clinched it for me. I knew I would have it. I thought this is for me.

When the woman began to have contractions I went to the hospital so that I could be there with her during the birth. We had made everything legal beforehand, so as soon as the baby was born the mother gave her straight to me. She never even knew that her baby was a girl. I said goodbye to her in the hospital and apart from one 'phone call never spoke to her again. She was a lovely woman, affectionate and kind; she never asked for anything and she kept her part of the bargain and never tried to contact the child. My husband was particularly worried that she would try to get in touch, but she never did.

We called the baby Rocio and she is the light of my life; she is recompense for all that we suffered with the other one. When she was three years old I started to tell her stories about her mother but in the form of a fairy tale, so she has always known that she was adopted. When she grew up I offered to help her trace her mother but she just told me not to be silly. She's twenty-six now and works as an economist.

It's funny because my life seems to have gone in parallels: I lost one wonderful husband only to find another one, equally wonderful; I adopted a monster of a child only to end up adopting another child who is an angel.

A woman in a mantilla

I truly believe that life contains both positives and negatives. In Seville they have a saying: *"En este mundo señores todo se paga"*, "In this life, gentlemen, you pay for everything." I believe you have to pay for everything, either before or after; I paid beforehand.'

Women and Charity

*"So faith, hope, charity, abide these three
But the greatest of these is charity." (Paul in the letter to the Corinthians)*

Spain is a Catholic country and to the Catholic Church charity is the theological virtue superior to all virtues. As one of the Apostles said: "If I ... have not charity, I am nothing."

Many of the women whose lives are recounted in this book did or do charity work: Maria helps the Nuevo Futuro; Lolina's mother spent all her life working for one charity or another, helping the nuns in the Red Cross Hospital in Melilla, joining the charity Obreras de la Cruz in Castellon and later, Madrid; Lui did not hesitate to contact the Message of Peace charity when she heard of an appeal on the radio and today works tirelessly for Manos Unidas. Even those women who did not join specific organisations felt it their duty to offer charity to those in need: Maria's mother refused to take a government pension; Lolina's grandmother gave money and food to those without and Paloma's grandmother saved food so that she could give it to the hungry. The Catholic Church preached charity and the women tried to live up to it. In the time of Franco, when the Church had greater influence over the family, it was expected that women of good families would become involved with some kind of charity work.

Nuevo Futuro
The Nuevo Futuro (New Future) charity was founded in 1968 by Carmen Herrero Garraldas to help abandoned children. The idea was not to become an alternative kind of orphanage

but to change and improve the system by which these children were looked after. There were two objectives: (i) to fight for the new legislation on the protection of the child and reform the Adoption Act and (ii) to create homes with a family environment in which the children could grow up, regardless of race or religion.

In 1986 the Government asked the association to reintegrate women prisoners with children under six years of age into the community. In 1988 Nuevo Futuro opened its first home for women prisoners with young children. The inmates and their children, although still under restrictions, received both social and work training to enable them to make an easier transition into normal life.

Today Nuevo Futuro has houses all over Spain helping children lead a better life and have a new future.

Manos Unidas
Since 1960, Manos Unidas, a Catholic charity has fought against poverty and hunger. In 2006 they had 833 projects in sixty-five countries; the majority of their work is in Third World countries.

Instituto Secular Obreras de la Cruz
The Catholic organisation, Instituto Secular Obreras de la Cruz, is a secular women's organisation devoted to doing good works. It was founded in 1923 by Vicente Garrido Pastor, a Doctor of Theology. In 1972 the branch Miembros Cooperadores was created for women without an evangelical calling but who lived in the spirit of the institution and shared its beliefs. Its aims were to promote social and Christian values, especially to the young. The institution runs hospitals,

schools, old people's homes, religious retreats and young people's summer camps.

BRIGITTE was born in Charleroi in 1956

Brigitte was born in Belgium but moved to Fuengirola in Spain with her parents in 1962 as a small child. She moved back to Belgium, joined the Belgian Air Force and eventually returned to Spain to work as a farmer. She lives with her partner, Isabel an internationally recognised painter and runs an internet company.

It was a difficult drive up through the old riverbed to Brigitte's farmhouse; recent rain had scoured away the soil and left deep ruts in the track and I had to proceed with caution. At last I arrived at the top and turned in towards the house, following signs that directed me to "Bambuzen" (Bamboo) and "Paint Ball". Brigitte owned 250,000 square metres of land and it all faced south, overlooking the Mediterranean. A number of scruffy, noisy dogs raced out to greet me and I sat apprehensively waiting in the car for someone to appear. At last a neat, compact woman with short, greying hair appeared; she wore sensible trousers and a thick sweater. Her handshake was warm and firm and with a "let's get down to it attitude" she soon had me sitting before a blazing log fire in the small room that constituted the main part of her house. The dogs had followed us inside and one was particularly interested in the smell of my trousers.

'He's a World Champion,' she said, pointing to the dog. 'I won the 1997 World Championship Dog Training competition in Torre del Mar with him. That was my passion for many years, dog training: defence, obedience and tracking. I loved it but I never did it as a job; I don't believe in earning money from animals.'

She stretched out her hand and stroked the dog.

'He's just a home dog now,' she added.

I suggested she begin by sketching out her background and she leaned back, pulled out a packet of strong smelling French cigarettes and proceeded to light one.

'Well my parents came to Spain back in 1962 and set up a business in Fuengirola. I was about six at the time and I went to the nearby French Lycée. I suppose I spent most of my formative years growing up in Spain, in Mijas. When I was sixteen my mother died and I went back to France to live with my father and sister. I wanted to finish my studies so I moved to Belgium and tried to get a grant to help me, but it was not easy. In the end I joined the Belgian Air Force. I was there for nine years, working as a trainer. They sent me to the United States to learn "Teaching Methodology" and then when I came back I began to run courses training members of the armed forces how to run their own training courses. I enjoyed the teaching part but then I got moved into an office and I did not like that so much; I felt it was too soon to be at a desk job so I left and returned to Spain.

My step-father had a vacant shop in Mijas so I rented it from him and set up business selling jewellery. After a while my brother came to Spain to join me and we opened a second shop. But two people in charge, that's one too many, so I decided to look for something else to do.

I met Jacqueline, a Frenchwoman, who had a strawberry farm in Torre del Mar and I started working with her. The problem with strawberries is that they do not grow well under plastic so they have a very short season: May, June and July. This is also the season when other European countries are producing their own strawberries so I suggested we turned some of the strawberries into finished products and sold them to shops and restaurants. I sold half my business to my brother and went into business with Jacqueline, making strawberry sorbets. We sold them to all the resorts along the coast. Then I decided to do varieties of salads, meszclum, we called them. Nowadays you can find mixed salads in the supermarkets but fifteen years ago it was a new idea that we brought from France. Then Jacqueline got divorced and we had to work harder with the strawberries but it was a bad time; by then the wages of the pickers were too high so Jacqueline sold her farm and I bought this one. The land here is not the same; it is much higher and it is not good for strawberry cultivation but by then I had a dream of growing bamboo. It was something I had wanted to do for a long time and I had tried growing a little of it at the other farm. So I bought fifty-five different varieties and planted them here. I normally sell the plants to construction companies for the gardens of their new developments but now the construction business has virtually stopped business is not good. And Spanish people are not spending money on their gardens at the moment. So I said to myself, OK, I must take another direction.

I have set up and opened three Paint Ball areas. We get groups of people of all ages, although not too young because it costs twenty, twenty-five euros a session. Usually there are between twelve and fifteen in a group. They may be friends or colleagues from a bank or solicitor's and they come for about three hours. I don't do much for companies yet because I would need to have enough activities to fill the whole day and so far I just have the Paint Ball. We divide the groups into two teams, provide them with masks and protective clothing and set them a task. Usually it's something simple like trying to capture the other side's flag but we have a variety of games for them to play. I sometimes use one of the old greenhouses for the Paint Ball; there's five thousand square metres in there.

There are four small houses on this piece of land; one for each of the women who live here. Jacqueline has a small studio in one; she is semi-retired now but still does the accounts for the business. Her daughter, Genevieve comes and lives here for six months of the year in another one. During the summer she works in France as a horse trainer, helping horses with behavioural problems. Basically what she tries to do is see things from the horse's point-of-view, which as you probably realise, is that of a prey animal. She is very successful. However when she's here she doesn't train our horses because the Spanish methods are very different to the French but she does help to look after them. Then Isabel, who is a painter, has one of the houses with her own studio and of course there is mine, this one, but with Isabel it's different: she and I live together, sometimes we live in her house and sometimes in mine. We all respect each other's privacy so it works very well and we have separate budgets for running the houses. Sometimes we eat together if we feel like it. It's a good arrangement because when you have a farm and animals it is difficult to go away on holiday; somebody always has to be there to look after things. I arrange my holidays when Genevieve or Jacqueline is here. That's usually in the winter but I don't mind; it's better than not having a holiday at all.'

She stopped to light another cigarette and chastise the dog in French for barking at a sudden sound then continued:

'The farm takes a lot of time; there's lots of work with the land, the horses and the dogs. I have tried growing other crops but it hasn't worked. It's OK if you have your family working here, like the Spanish do, because you don't have to pay Social Security. I pay Social Security for all my guys and it's expensive. When we were growing strawberries I employed over thirty men, all Spanish, never immigrants. Now I just employ two. I don't like to work with Arabs and it's mainly Arab immigrants that work in the fields. It's just that I know how Spanish country people think and I find it easier to work with them.'

I asked her if she had any other business interests in Spain.

'Yes, the *Centro Comercial*,' she said, pointing behind her at her computer.

When I looked perplexed she explained:

'It's an on-line shopping centre set up in the French area and I'm currently working with a Canadian company to develop a Spanish version of it. It's a multi-level system with over two thousand shops; you can buy anything: tickets, clothes, food, car hire, hotel rooms, everything. We offer discounts to customers to retain customer loyalty and we network with other websites. For me it's a retirement plan actually. It's not a way of making money quickly but it will gradually build up. I get commission every time someone buys something. It's new to Spain and we'll be introducing it into England soon as well.'

She exhaled contentedly and added:

'The Spanish people don't like to serve you. I always feel that I am disturbing them. Even if you want to buy a car they will not make an effort to serve you. Personally I don't have any problem with Spanish people because I grew up here and I speak fluent Spanish but having said that I will always be a stranger here. After ten or twelve years here you begin to feel a need to speak your own language, to be with people from your own background and to eat your own food. But when you live away from your own country for so long you are also a stranger in your own country; you are from nowhere. You become a nomad. Once you have moved from your country one time it is easy to do it again but you will never belong to Spain; you will always be a "*guiri*", a foreigner. It's not just here, it's everywhere. You acquire your deep habits, your culture if you like, between the age of one and six; that's what you are.

When I first came back here in 1985 I was fascinated by the Spanish culture, especially the Flamenco, but now I have lost interest. I used to have many Spanish friends but now I have fewer. Then two years ago I decided I would join a French Association and meet French people. I needed it. We meet; we exchange books; we eat together. I read perfect Spanish but I feel in French. Spanish people don't have the same way of thinking in associations as French people; they don't have the long tradition of working together in associations without any financial involvement. When I was doing the dog training I was very involved with the Spanish team; I represented Spain in the World Championships; I was a judge and a trainer. But after ten years I became tired with it. I had given a lot: time, money, provided the field for the competitions, all free. But it was not appreciated; what is free has no value here. It would have been better to have charged them. In the end I stopped and told them to do it all themselves.'

A car drove slowly up the drive and she looked up to see who it was then continued:

'Spain has changed a lot since I was a child. I grew up here in the Franco era but I was young and not politically minded so I was not aware of any hardships. I remember there was no crime, no pickpockets, you could leave your door unlocked. I know some Spanish people have bad memories of those days but I have good memories. Now it has changed; everybody has a television, a car, more money but I don't think their lives are any better. I'm not sure. As I said I was sixteen when I left Spain. The schools in France were very political in those days and everyone thought it was very bad to be living in Spain under Franco; but I didn't think that. In 1968 everything was opening up to the outside world. It was good for the foreigners; it was very cheap and you hardly had to pay any taxes. Even if you only had a little money it seemed a lot here. When we came to Mijas we had some Canadian friends who bought some land at half a peseta a square metre; now that land is worth fifteen thousand pesetas a square metre. If you arrived with French francs or Canadian dollars you had money to start a business even though they still charged the foreigners more. My parents had a shop in Mijas; I remember one day that a coach-load of American tourists arrived and they bought everything in the shop. There was nothing left even though my parents overcharged them. Lots of foreigners came to the coast then for their holidays; British girls and topless bathing made a big impact. There were lots of changes but many were superficial. Many of the Spanish *campesinos* owned land that had no value; it had no water; it was no good for growing anything, not even for supporting goats. Then they found that the foreigners liked their land because it had a nice view and so they began to sell it. It's a bit like this land,' she said, waving her arm towards the fields. 'Very poor soil but I know I will always be able to sell it because it has a magnificent view.'

I remembered the drive up to the farm and nodded my agreement.

'People had a simple life in those days and we have changed that. When I was first in Mijas people did not sit indoors watching television; they had no television. They sat outside their front doors, in the street, talking to their neighbours and friends. Nowadays they are inside with the air-conditioning and the television on. The people used to be so generous. They never had very much but that did not stop them giving you some grapes or a few avocados or maybe some tomatoes. Now they want to sell you everything. The people do not seem to be so happy anymore; they are more closed and even bored with the foreigners. Maybe they are resentful that houses have become so expensive because of us.

Of course the lives of women in the cities are different from those in the country, where tradition is still very strong and even though they don't all believe in the Catholic Church anymore they still do things the old way. In the country young people are expected to get married; they are together four or five years to earn the money then they marry. In the city it's like elsewhere in the world they just live together. I have two young guys working for me; they live in the small hamlet of Los Iberos. All the people in that hamlet are related, cousins. Both men have married girls from Los Iberos and followed the same traditions of twenty years ago.

I'm a Catholic. Well I mean that I was baptised and confirmed in the Catholic Church because my parents were Catholics. I was educated by nuns in a convent in Belgium. But actually I am an agnostic; I don't really believe in religion. I am quite interested in Buddhism; I like the idea that you have to find the Way and maybe you'll find Him there rather than "You have to believe first and then you will find Him." I am not a Buddhist. I find it interesting but it is not my culture. What I do like is the idea that you have to work on yourself and maybe there is something at the end of it.

Here in Spain there is still a weight to religion although the priest is no longer so important. They have Christ on the bedroom wall, medallions, Semana Santa but they don't go to church.'

Lesbians, Homosexuals and Gay marriage

After years of oppression during the rule of Franco Spain has become one of the most open societies in the world in respect of the rights of Gays, Lesbians, Bisexuals and Transgender people. Under Franco the existing Vagrancy Act was amended in 1954 to declare homosexuality illegal and to equate it with proxenetism. The Act stated that the law was not intended to punish but to "correct and reform" those that had "fallen to the lowest levels of morality". Homosexuals, mostly men, were imprisoned in special prisons called "galerias de invertidos" (deviant galleries). It is thought that the poet Federico Garcia Lorca was murdered as much for being a homosexual as for his political beliefs. However despite being outlawed many Gays and Lesbians were able to meet in clandestine gay bars during the 1960s, especially in Barcelona. The Vagrancy Act was eventually repealed in 1979.

In 2004 the General Council of the Judiciary agreed that existing discrimination against homosexuals could not be tolerated but did not go so far as to condone same-sex marriage. Then under the administration of the Socialist government of 2005 homosexuals were allowed to have the same rights as other citizens including the right to marry and adopt children. On July 11th 2005 two Gay men were married under new legislation that allowed same sex marriage. Eleven days later the first Lesbian couple were married. The reaction of the Catholic Church was immediate and clear, saying that this legislation was an attack on family values. Pope Benedict XVI was quoted as saying that "According to human nature it is man and woman who are made for each other and give humanity a future." The Prime Minister José

Luis Zapatero responded by denying that allowing same-sex marriages damaged families; on the contrary he said that "this law recognises and values marriage." He added that: "A society that avoids senseless suffering of its citizens is a better society." During the first year after the law was passed 4,500 same-sex couples were married in Spain and fifty petitions for adoption were made.

In November 2006 the law on assisted reproduction was amended allowing the non-biological mother to be recognised as a parent as well as the mother who gave birth to the child.

Shortly after the law was passed issues were raised regarding the validity of a same-sex marriage between a Spaniard and a foreigner. It was clarified that at least one partner must be a Spanish citizen or both should have legal residence in Spain for the marriage to be legal.

ANA was born in Madrid in 1954

Ana was born in Madrid, the daughter of a High Court judge and trained to be a doctor. She is married, has two daughters and works at a hospital in Málaga as an anaesthetist.

Ana, unlike many Spaniards, is always punctual and at six o'clock precisely she arrived at my house, her face wreathed in smiles. At first she had been reluctant to talk to me but later admitted that she had lived through a very interesting time in Spanish history and it would like to tell me about it.

'I was at university in Madrid in 1972, in the last years of the dictatorship. Things were very difficult then; Franco's regime was in decline and there was a great deal of social unrest. So much so that even Franco felt he had to loosen his hold on the country a little. There was no official movement for change; it was all clandestine: secret meetings in the university, on street corners, in cafes. We had no freedom and the government would not let us do anything; everything was strictly controlled by the police. I was in the Faculty of Medicine where we had to study very hard, so there wasn't much time for anything else, but in some of the other faculties, particularly the arts, history and law, the students were more interested in politics than studying. There were lots of student leaders who weren't there to study but to try to bring about political change; the entire university was taken over by politics. During my first year, in an attempt to stop these meetings, the government closed the university down from November. We were not allowed to go to any classes but we could take the exams in June if we wanted. It was impossible to study without any instruction. When we arrived to take the exams we went into the exam room in single file, walking between two lines of *Grises*, that's what we called the police because of their grey uniforms,' she added. 'I had a pen in one hand and my identity card in the other; nothing else was allowed. Of course most of us failed. I managed to retake my exams later, two in June and two in September, but it was hard.

Then there were the *soplones*, the members of the *Ligada Politica Social*, who were posing as students, but actually were working for the police. They would contact the police as soon as they knew about any meetings or demonstrations. The police took a very hard line, especially after the ETA bombing of Carrero Blanco, the Prime Minister and the man chosen as Franco's successor, in 1973. At the time everyone applauded the assassination; in those days ETA was a group of people like everyone else who just wanted freedom from the regime. So when the government shot a number of political prisoners in a village outside Madrid it caused an international outcry. Although the men admitted to killing Carrero Blanco nobody thought the government had the right to shoot the prisoners. Things began to escalate from then on.

People were not allowed to gather into groups of more than three because they said that that meant they were having a meeting. If the police saw you they would come and split the group up. Behind the university was a mountain and beyond that was the Hospital Civil. I remember vividly running away from the police who were chasing us, some of them on horseback. It was terrifying trying to climb the mountain, everyone running and the police lashing out at us. We were desperate to get into Madrid so we could disperse and evade them. It was a time of great fear especially for us students. One time I hid for four hours in the bathroom, sitting on top of the toilet seat so that nobody could see my feet under the door. I can't tell you how frightened I was.

When they came into the university you hid anywhere you could. It didn't matter if you were guilty of anything or not, you were still beaten. The police would position themselves in the doorways and use their batons to hit at anyone who went past. The worst part was when people you knew began to disappear. For example you would hear someone speak one night at a meeting and the next day he'd be gone. I was in the basketball team and one of the team, a very left-wing student disappeared. After four months he reappeared; he'd been locked up and badly beaten and he still had bruises and seemed out of it, dazed almost.

Of course we were all young then; at eighteen we were very idealistic and left-wing. We wanted democracy and to be rid of the dictatorship, so we fought against Franco. We had no freedom to speak out or to criticise the regime; there was strict censorship of everything: cinemas, books, newspapers, television. Nobody knew what was happening in the world or even what was happening in Spain. Even in the cinema, instead of having a normal newsreel we had *Noticiarios Españoles, los Nodos* we called them, which always opened with the Spanish flag blowing in the breeze, a picture of Franco and a background of stirring music. Then you would sit and watch Franco opening a new reservoir or his daughter or his wife doing something; no news, just a week in the life of Franco. There were no open debates at government level or any other. On the 1st May, Labour Day, each year they would put two football matches and a bullfight on the television so that people would stay at home and not go out onto the streets and demonstrate.

Besides my friends in the Faculty of Medicine I also had friends in other faculties, law and literature. In general they didn't study as hard as we did; they didn't need to, so they enjoyed life more and spent almost all their time in meetings discussing the fate of the regime. They would call me and say "Come over this evening there's a good film in such-and-such faculty." It would be a banned film of course. Other times we would hand around copies of banned books, "The sayings of Chairman Mao" for example. I never went to anyone's house for meetings and they never came to my house because my father was a judge and very right-wing.

Ana (far left) and student friends

In my time there were lots of women in university but almost all from the middle-class. The sort of school I went to encouraged you to have a university education. In the Faculty of Medicine the course was six years: three years in the university then three working in a hospital. You could request to go to a particular hospital but it was mostly down to chance; first of all I trained in the university hospital but then my brother, who was a professor at the university, pulled some strings for me and I got transferred to a hospital in the centre of Madrid. It was much better and the classes were smaller. That was where I met my husband, Eduardo, when we were in the fifth year, although we didn't start going out together until we had finished the course.

When I finished my studies I had to present myself for the national examinations in order to get on a specialist course. I wanted to be an anaesthetist which meant another four years of study. When I had finished those four years I had to take another national exam in order to get a position. Then, depending on the results of the exam, I could choose the hospital I wanted to work in. The people with the highest results got to choose first. Eduardo was doing his military service by then, so we waited a year until he finished then we chose together, so we would get the same hospital. We chose Málaga.

It's difficult to move from hospital to hospital nowadays because of the autonomous regions; I don't think I would be able to move to Galicia for example without losing my permanent position. And of course I'd have to do another national exam.'

She stopped, smiled to herself then continued:

'In my student days my father, who was very rich, gave me an allowance of six hundred pesetas a week; Eduardo's parents gave him two thousand a week. I remember when I came home waving my *papelita*s, saying to my father: "I'm a doctor now, Papi", he congratulated me and then said: "Well, now you know you have to earn your own living." And he didn't give me my six hundred pesetas anymore. He wasn't mean, he always said I could ask for anything I wanted, but I never did. If I needed more money I worked by giving classes.

I got on well with my father; we never argued except once over religion and we never discussed politics. He was born in Seville in 1902, the son of a famous army officer who owned a great deal of land. He had seven sisters and one brother. He and his brother were sent to Pamplona to study law at a Jesuit university but they never expected to work as lawyers; they expected to be landowners and work on their land. They had acres of land for hunting and breeding horses. I'm not sure what else they used the land for, but I know my father had a very privileged life style. He told me that he could ride before he could walk. Also he had the very first motor car in Andalusia. He knew how to live the good life.

My mother was from Santander but her father was also a judge and it was during his posting to Seville that my mother met my father. My father asked her father if he could marry her and my grandfather, who was a very strict man, asked him how he intended to support her. My father was surprised at the question and said that he did not need to work that he had all their land to live on. But my grandfather did not think that was enough and persuaded my father to apply for a job as a judge. So my father began his career as a judge and left the land in the hands of his brother, who managed it very badly and lost it all to the Reds during the Civil War. All the children, except my father, became penniless and even after the war the land was never returned to the family.

Being a judge in those days meant living in a lot of different places. When you wanted promotion it usually meant a move. My father was a judge in Almeria, where two of my siblings were born then he moved to Cordoba, where another two were born and I was born in Madrid. Each job was more important than the previous one and in the end he was a *Magistrado* on the *Tribunal Superior de Justicia*. Legal appointments in Spain are not political appointments; they are independent, but having said that he would not have risen so high under Franco's government if he had not been very right-wing.

Ana's father with his friend the Countess of Altazar, 1943

During the Civil War my father was in La Rambla, near Cordoba, when the Republicans took the village. They surrounded his house and he could see the soldiers outside playing cards for my mother; they planned to kill my father and rape my mother. My father had a gun with five bullets in it; he told my mother there was a bullet each for her and the children and one for him. He stayed like that for a couple of days before the Nationalist troops arrived and liberated the village. Just as well or I wouldn't be here now.

Ana's christening

My childhood was a little unusual; for a start my mother was forty-seven when I was born, a gap of sixteen years after my sister. So I had more in common with my nieces and my cousins' children than my own brother and sisters; my elder sister was more like a second mother to me. I was always the black sheep of the family, but I think this was partly because I lived in a different generation and my mother had died when I was only ten years old so my father brought me up. One of my sisters is mentally challenged, so for many years the three of us: my father, me and her, lived together with two maids to help us. My father always said I had to grow up quickly then, but my sisters reckoned I was spoilt and that he let me do what I wanted. My father retaliated by saying that he had confidence that I would always do the right thing. He was rather too old to bring me up, I suppose. The joke was that I didn't have to do the usual social service that women were obliged to do at that time because I had a widowed father to look after. In fact I had far less to do than most of my friends; I never even had to make my bed.

Of course when I married it was different and I had a lot to learn and there was no mother to teach me. My elder sister lived in Huelva by then; she was married to a judge so they too had to move about a lot during their married life. She would have helped but she was always too far away. I think the emancipation of women is misunderstood; I found married life quite a change.'

'Do you see much difference between your younger years and those of your daughters?' I asked.

She has two daughters, one working and one still in university.

'No, not as much as you think; not as much difference as there was between my generation and my sisters. There's the technology of course, but otherwise I did much the same things as they do now: I went on holiday with my friends; I had a car; I went camping in the Sierra. I had quite a bit of freedom. My elder daughter lives with her boyfriend and Eduardo and I lived together for a few months but then we decided to get married to please my father.

I don't mind if my daughter doesn't get married; in fact I thinks it is better she doesn't. Even if she wanted to marry she can't marry in church because she isn't baptised. Neither of our daughters are baptised; we don't believe in it. It caused a lot of problems with my family because they are all very religious, very traditional and very conservative; one of my nieces is a nun. It was quite a fight. Then when the children went to school it was one battle after another over religious instruction. Spain's a Catholic country so it was mandatory but you could opt to study ethics instead if you had a good reason. But I felt my daughters were discriminated against; sometimes they would be the only ones in the ethics class and there would be no proper classroom for them. I sometimes wondered why I bothered; it would have been easier to have let them go with their friends, but my principles wouldn't allow it. Then there was the problem of the first communion. I asked them why do you want to take communion, because of the party or because you want to talk to God? They were only eight years old so of course they said because of the party. I gave them a swimming pool party and they invited all their class and everyone brought them presents. So we were all happy. I could not stand in the church and promise to bring my daughters up in the Catholic faith when I had no intention of doing so. I know many people do but I couldn't.

I had been raised in a very Catholic family so it wasn't easy for me to give up the church; I thought about it long and hard before I decided. I was at university at the time. I think the Catholic Church has caused so much suffering and damage over the years and there is so much money involved. I'm not in agreement with it at all; I couldn't believe in something like that. If anything the Protestant Church is better, less fuss, less ceremony. Nowadays I'm still against the Church but I am more confused; I'm not against the idea of God only the Church. Eduardo doesn't believe in anything but I think it's nice to believe that there is something when we die. I have always thought that my mother was there, watching over me, protecting me. I know if you rationalise it it's not possible, but I still like to think it.'

The Universities and Student Unrest

Until the mid-nineteenth century Spanish universities were run and controlled by the Government; each faculty was headed by one man, the Catedratico, who held the professional chair and wielded supreme authority over all teaching. In the 1960s the number of university students increased from 76,000 to 213,000 but the structure and facilities of the universities remained the same. Students became impatient with overcrowded classrooms and outdated methods of teaching. This was a time of student unrest in Spain as well as elsewhere in Europe; Madrid and Barcelona became regular scenes of protest marches and demonstrations. The government's response to any dissension was immediate and hard. In May 1966, 1,500 students took part in a march at the University of Madrid and were met by riot police and baton charges; 50 students were arrested. In January 1967, after further student demonstrations, ten universities were closed and eleven demonstrators were arrested. The students continued demonstrating throughout April and May and in October joined up with intellectuals and professional workers in support of the workers' demonstrations; several hundred were arrested by the police and many were injured. The unrest continued throughout the year and in December the students at Madrid University called for a strike until all those arrested were released. In January of the following year the Government responded by closing the Faculty of Social Science and Economy, confiscating the students' admission fees and forcing them to reapply for admission. The violence continued and there were frequent clashes between the police and the students. By the middle of January 1968, the riots were so bad that the police took over the campus, moving in with 35 riot vehicles, horses and water cannons. All the faculties were closed and students were obliged to reapply for admission. At the end of January, the Government decided to use special police agents as informers at the university. In February there were further riots and clashes with the police. The violence continued and, in April the Government appointed a more liberal Minister of Education, a member of the Catholic organisation Opus Dei.

The new Spanish Constitution of 1978 stated that the universities had the right to be autonomous but it was not until 1983 that the University Reform Law, whose main aim was to provide an equal opportunity for all Spaniards to have a university education, was implemented. The law decentralised the control of the universities, moving it into the hands of social councils which were coordinated nationally by a National University Council. Each university had four administrative bodies: a university council, a governing body, the faculties' council and a department council.

During the 1980s the number of female students at university increased but women were not represented in all the academic areas. The professions that had always attracted women, such as pharmacy, education and journalism were the most popular. Nevertheless by 1984, 47% of all students were female. In 1994 over a million students were enrolled in universities.

Spanish universities fall into two groups: private and State. Private universities are either Catholic or run by private organisations; the majority of universities are State run.

DOLORES MARIA (LOLI) was born in Barcelona in 1973

Loli is married and has one daughter. She trained as a physiotherapist and went to work in Toledo; she now works in the hospital in Velez Málaga. She grew up the daughter of an officer of the Guardia Civil. She has strong religious beliefs but is not a member of the Catholic Church.

When I hurt my shoulder some months ago, the doctor recommended that I go for a course of physiotherapy. 'Ask for Loli,' my friend whispered in my ear. 'She's wonderful.'

Each evening as I lay face up on the treatment table, allowing only the slightest of moans to escape my lips as Loli manipulated my arm through 360 degrees, I listened to her tell me a little of her life:

'When I finished my training I wanted to apply for a permanent post here in Velez Málaga, but there was nothing at all available in Andalusia. I could have got a temporary position, but that would have meant waiting years for a full-time contract, so I applied for a job in Toledo. Once I had my contract I planned to ask for a transfer to a hospital in Andalusia, but I then found out that transfers were taking up to seven years to come through. Of course by then it was too late to change my mind, so I worked in Toledo for a year. It is a beautiful city, but I was very lonely. I had just got married and I couldn't wait to go home each weekend to see Alejandro, my husband. He's a physiotherapist too; we graduated at the same time, but he was much luckier than me and got a placement in this hospital right away. Well I began to think that I could not carry on living apart from him for very much longer when I found out that I was pregnant. I moved back to Velez-Málaga and my daughter, Maria was born.

The government allows you three years maternity leave and lets you include them in your years of service, so I decided to take advantage of that and stay at home and look after my baby for three years.

Turn on your left side,' she instructed me, pummelling my muscles with her capable hands. Loli was a small woman, with bird-like bones that denied their real strength. Her face was thin and perfectly balanced and her eyes were a warm grey; she wore her hair long and frizzy and its natural dark brown had been streaked with blonde. She continued with her story:

'Well when Maria, my daughter was nearly three and I had to go back to work, I tried to get something closer to home. At first there was nothing and I was on the point of moving back to Toledo, and taking Maria with me, when a temporary post was advertised in Torrox. It was only about half an hour away, so I applied for it and I worked there for three years. Then my transfer came up; it wasn't to Velez-Málaga, but it was in Andalusia. I had a permanent post at last, in Antequerra, a beautiful, old town in the mountains. I enjoyed working at the hospital; it was well organised, I had my three treatment beds and there was plenty of equipment, but the journey was horrific. It was eighty kilometres each way and took me about fifty minutes. I stuck it out for a few months until I heard about the job here; it's not permanent, but at least I'm only five minutes from home now. Maybe next year I'll get a permanent transfer.'

She slapped some clear gel on my shoulder and proceeded to use the ultra-son machine. The rhythmic circular massage was soothing.

'It's so much easier to organise our lives now that we are working in the same hospital. Alejandro works the morning shift and I work the afternoon one. I get up in the morning, get my daughter ready and take her to school then I prepare the lunch and the dinner for the evening. In the summer I go to the beach every day; I swim, I meditate and then I read my book before going home to eat. When it is too cold to swim, I just sit on the beach and meditate or read. I love the sea; it reminds me of God, it is so vast. For me it's important to have some quiet time each day to reflect; I need my solitude and I need to be out in the open air, either in the country or by the sea. I hate being inside all the time, and when the weather is not good enough to go out I feel very depressed. My shift never finishes before nine o'clock each night and then I go home and have dinner, but twice a week I go straight to my yoga class instead.'

She gave my shoulder a yank and added:

'It would do you good to go to yoga. You should think about it; it's very good for your posture.'

I muttered some agreement. She continued:

'Alejandro is very good; he helps me a lot in the flat: he does the shopping, he dusts and he does the ironing. He is studying osteopathy now in his spare time as well. It's a good arrangement because he gets to spend lots of time with Maria and helps her with her schoolwork. I wish I could spend more time with her, but it's difficult. In the summer I take her to the beach every morning and of course we have the weekends. She is learning the catechism at the moment, because it's her first communion soon. I would like to help her with it, but I'm always at work and she is in bed when I get home, so Alejandro helps her.

Maria made her own choice to take the first communion; I told her it was up to her, but that she was not to choose to do it just because of the presents, like lots of the kids do. I said if she took her first communion it was something special between her and God and that when she was older she would also have to be confirmed. She knows she is not getting any presents, nor are we buying her a fancy dress. Of course she will have a nice dress, but nothing elaborate. I want her to realise that this is an important decision she is making. In the weeks leading up to their first communion the children are expected to attend Mass each Sunday, but she says that some of her friends' parents won't let them go. They want them to take their communion because it's traditional but don't want them to go to church each week.'

She turned off the machine and wiped the gel from my arm.

'I'm not keen on all the regalia of the church; I suppose I am more Lutheran than Catholic in my attitude. We go to Mass every Sunday morning then afterwards we sing with some of the youngsters and Alejandro plays the guitar. Sunday is also the day for getting together with the Christian association that we belong to. This is something we have set up ourselves and we pray and meditate and discuss all sorts of issues: ethical and religious. There are nine of us: four couples and a woman whose husband is not interested in joining. Sometimes we go away together to a retreat for a few days; next weekend is the Feast of St. Pilar and it's a Bank Holiday weekend so on Friday morning we are going to Alhama de Granada. We will stay in a big house that belongs to a convent; there are only four nuns in the convent now, and they are all very old. As it is a cloistered order the nuns never go outside; they are almost self sufficient and have their own vegetable garden and an orchard of fruit trees. Years ago they used to make sweet cakes and sell them, but their oven is broken now. If they need anything, like bread, someone comes from the town and places it in the *torno*, a kind of shuttered window that operates on a turntable. The food is placed on the turntable in the window opening and it is turned round to the nuns' side so they can take it out. In that way no-one can see them and they can't see anyone.

We take the children with us; our group has seven between us, so that's great for Maria, she has plenty of friends to play with. The women prepare some food beforehand and that way we don't have to spend all our time cooking. I'm taking some Russian salad and a beef stew. I hope they turn out alright; I'm not used to cooking for so many people.'

One day she decided to tell me about her childhood:
'I was actually born in Barcelona, you know, but we moved to Málaga when I was only six months old, so I think of myself as Malagueña. My father was a member of the Guardia Civil and he had to move about quite a bit; my sister was born in Alicante and my youngest brother was born in Málaga. For the first few years of my life we lived in the c*uarteles,* the married quarters that adjoined the police station. It was a very enclosed community made up solely of the families of the Guardia Civil and we used to have parties and celebrate the feast days together, especially St. Pilar, the patron saint of the Guardia Civil. There were lots of other children living there, so I had plenty of friends and despite the fact that our apartment was tiny, we always had lots of places to play. There was a family of stray cats living inside the courtyard and each of the children adopted one to look after. One day a big, black dog got into the compound and killed

mine. There was nothing I could do except stand and watch; I remember being very upset and I suppose that was when I first began to think about death. Three days later my mother told me that one of the neighbour's children had leukaemia and was going to die. Somehow the two things have become linked in my memory.

When I was seven my father had to leave the Guardia Civil; he had been suffering from depression and couldn't be trusted to carry a loaded gun. It was an enormous change for me because I had to leave all my friends, change schools and move to a new home. We moved to an even smaller flat near the old tobacco factory, right by the sea. I hated it there: the constant noise of the sea frightened me and when I had to walk home it was always so dark and lonely. I became a very depressed child at that time.

Then when I was fourteen my parents separated and I and my brothers and sister went to live with my mother. My parents never divorced and neither of them has remarried since. My mother is seventy now and my father is a little older. My mother was always a very traditional wife and mother; she did everything for my father.'

She laughed and added:

'It's a good job I was born in 1973 and not in that era because I don't think I would have been able to keep my mouth shut.'

'What about your grandparents?' I asked.

'I don't remember them very much, although I do remember once when my grandmother had to go into hospital, she packed her shroud and a pillow in case she died.'

A woman on the next treatment bed laughed and added:

'Well my grandmother did the same thing when she went on her honeymoon.'

This caused a ripple of laughter around the room and people began to relate their own versions of this custom. When the chatter died down Loli continued:

'It's our tenth wedding anniversary on Friday,' she told me with a smile. 'You know I'm very lucky to have met Alejandro. We get on so well. Each year we give each other a special present, nothing expensive, but always something with a lot of sentiment. This year I'm making a collage of photos for him, one from each year of our marriage, and I'm putting a drawing round each one to typify that particular year. But it's taking me ages and I don't know if it will be finished in time. I have to work on it when he is not at home and I haven't a lot of time. Last year he made me a computer presentation of photos and music, using Powerpoint. It was lovely; I was so pleased with it. Another year he made me a CD of the songs he had composed; they are all about us and our life together. He is very talented and he has a lovely voice.'

The clinic was almost empty by then, so she left me for a moment to put a copy of his songs on the CD player. Her husband's strong, clear voice floated over us, singing of his love for his young wife. I closed my eyes and relaxed.

Women of the Spanish "Generation of 27"

The Generation of 27 was the name given to an influential group of poets, writers, philosophers, musicians and artists that formed part of Spain's literary and intellectual circle in the years 1923 to 1927. Their first meeting was in Seville and after that a number of other centres were formed: in Madrid, Málaga and Tenerife. Most of the members were men but a number of distinguished women belonged: Ernestina de Champourcín, Concha Mendez, Maruja Mallo, Pilar de Valderrama, Elisabeth Mulder, Rosa Chacel, Josefina de la Torre, Consuelo Berges, Rosa Garcia Ascot, Matilde de la Torre and María Zambrano. The onset of the Civil War split the movement; many were forced into exile, Federico Lorca was murdered and others were arrested. Although each had his or her own distinctive style one common theme was the link between Spanish popular culture and folklore.

Ernestina de Champoucin *was a poet and writer. She lived in exile from 1936 until 1972.*

Rosa Garcia Ascot *was a pianist and composer. She went into exile in 1939 and returned to Madrid in 1965 when she retired from public life. She died in 2002 at the age of 100.*

Maria Zambrano *was a Spanish essayist and philosopher, who was influenced by the writings of the Spanish philosopher Jose Ortega y Gasset. She taught Metaphysics at Madrid University until the outbreak of the Spanish Civil War. Her involvement in the war led to her exile under the Franco regime. She returned to Spain in 1984 and died in 1991 aged 87.*

Concha Mendez *was a poet, dramatist and scriptwriter. She was born in 1898 and died in 1986. Her work was influenced by a number of her colleagues such as the poets Lorca and Alberti. She met the writer Consuelo Berges, who befriended her.*

Consuelo Berges *was born in Santander in 1899. She became a reporter for the local newspaper "La Region" then in 1927 moved to Peru and then to Argentina. She returned to Spain in 1931 attracted by the ideas of the new Republic and took up work on the national newspaper "El Sol". At the end of the war she fled to France where she stayed until 1944. She translated the works of Stendhal, Proust and Flaubert into Spanish. She died in 1988.*

Matilde de la Torre *was a Socialist, a schoolteacher and an author. She was well educated in Greek and Latin, spoke a number of modern languages, played the piano, and conducted the school choir. In 1928 she wrote "Don Quijote, King of Spain", a history of Spanish decadence. Her writing was influenced by the ideas of the Spanish philosopher Jose Ortega y Gasset. She lived most of her life in exile in Mexico.*

Josefina de la Torre *was a poet, born in Gran Canaria in 1907. She moved to Madrid in 1927 where she lived until 1935. One of her most famous collections of poetry is called "Poemas de la Isla".*

Rosa Chacel *was born in 1898 in Valladolid. She was a novelist. She moved to Brazil at the end of the Civil War where she lived until 1977 when her husband died and she* *returned to Spain. In 1987 she received the "National Award of Letters" which is presented to the best writer in Spain. Then in 1990 she was awarded the "Premio Castilla y Leon de las Letras" by King Juan Carlos. She died in 1994.*

Elisabeth Mulder *was born in Barcelona in 1904. She was a poet, writer of children's books and a translator from her native Catalan into Spanish. She died in 1987.*

Pilar de Valderrama *was born in 1892 in Madrid. Although she was a poet she is better remembered for being the muse of a famous poet of the day. Although she was married and had three children, Antonio Machado fell deeply in love with her and for ten years he wrote to her, seeking her opinions, asking her advice and declaring his love for her in prose and verse.*

LUZ was born in Málaga in 1982

Luz was born in Málaga, the elder daughter of two doctors. She is single and lives with her boyfriend. She went to university in Málaga and obtained a degree in Publicity and Public Relations. She also has a Masters in Marketing and speaks perfect English. She works as a dental receptionist in Málaga. She has a sister who is still at university.

Luz was an attractive, well educated, modern young woman. She had a degree in Publicity and Public Relations, a Masters in Marketing and spoke perfect English.

She was currently working as a receptionist in a dental surgery. I asked her if she thought that job opportunities had improved for women.

'Things are very bad at the moment; there are no jobs for men or women. Even though there are more women than men in the universities, 60% to 40%, it's the same for both. No-one can find work in their specialism. I'm planning to do another Masters, Marketing within the Health Service. Even if we do have a recession there will still be lots of health clinics and hospitals opening; I think it will be a good area to work in.

Where I think there is a difference between men and women at the more senior levels, when you want to move up and get some promotion. Most of the existing bosses are men and a bit *machista*, but that too is changing. People recognise that men are good at certain things and women at others; for example women are very good at organisation. I think women make good managers. I believe things are changing but it's still quite difficult for women; although personally, in the short time I have been working, I have never had any problems because I am a woman.

The government are doing a lot to help women these days; I think that is fine for middle-aged women, especially if they have their own businesses, but I think it is ridiculous for the government to give all the help to women and nothing to men. That is only going to provoke feminism. Extremes are bad; they shouldn't favour one sex over the other but should choose the person according to their merit.'

'Have your qualifications been of use to you?' I asked her.

'Well I'm a bit annoyed with the government because I think they have prepared us badly. Here in Spain everyone thinks their children should go to university and nobody is interested in vocational training. Even though you might have other ideas on what you want to do you are expected to get your degree. Not everyone can be a judge or a doctor or go to university. And now look what's happened; there are lots of people out of work. I studied for seven years and I don't use any of it in my work at the moment. It was a waste of seven years; well not all of it I suppose, the cultural side was useful.

Today employers expect you to have a degree for whatever job. They won't even interview you if you haven't got a degree. When I worked in the sports store they said that having studied for my degree showed that I was a responsible person. I don't think it is right. In my case for example I would have liked to do something practical, something with my hands, but I never had the chance. Now I think I would have liked to have been a vet or a doctor but I can't retrain now, not after seven years. I just don't fancy it; I prefer to continue with the marketing. It's a shame because I don't really like what I'm doing, me and thousands of other Spaniards. Do you know all the friends that studied Public Relations with me are now graphic designers. They did a short course on how to use the software and then went to work as graphic designers.

I think that when children are fourteen or fifteen they should do a psychological test to see where their aptitudes lie. It's not enough to let them say, "Oh I like Maths so I'll do something with Maths." They need to know what work they will be good at.

It's sad because there are lots like me who are disillusioned because they've studied, got their degree and now have no job. But then I remember that there's a crisis in Spain; there's no work at any level.'

'Have you thought about going to another country to work? After all you speak excellent English,' I asked.

'Yes, I have thought about it but I like it here in Málaga; I like the quality of life. It's much tougher in England or Holland.'

She had won an Erasmus scholarship to study for six months in Holland as part of her degree.

'What about your boyfriend?'

'We've talked about going abroad together to work, but he's very happy with the work he has here. He's a motor mechanic for specialist rally cars. His father was a well known rally driver.

Carlos is great; we get on really well. We've been living together now for two years but we have known each other a lot longer because we belonged to the same group of friends. When we started to go out together it didn't take long before we decided to live together. We moved into a flat that used to belong to his grandparents; they left it to him and his sister when they died. We pay his sister some rent every month for her share of it. Actually we would like to buy it from her but she won't sell. She's like *el perro del hortelano, que ni come ni deja comer*, the dog who guards the vegetable garden; he doesn't want to eat the vegetables but won't let you eat them either. But I can't say anything; she's his sister. It's a lovely flat, right in the centre of Málaga and very convenient for us to get to work. I can get to the surgery on my moped.

My parents didn't mind me moving in with Carlos. I suppose it was because when I came back from Holland I had changed a lot of my ideas on life. I thought to myself, why am I still living at home? It's very common in Spain for children to live at home until they're in their thirties but I don't think it's a good idea. It's not that I don't like my parents; I just think I should stand on my own two feet, be independent. In Europe everyone leaves home at a much younger age. It's ridiculous to keep living with your parents. Now I get on really well with them; I go to see them because I want to, not because I have to. When I lived at home I always felt on edge; I didn't like to cause any arguments, so I'd be really tense about everything. I was always quarrelling with my sister because we shared a bedroom; now we get on really well. When I got my first job at the sports store I had a good wage; I gave a little to my mother and the rest was for me. Now it's different; by the time I pay all the bills I have about 10% left for me.'

'Do you think your parents would like you to marry?'

'It's all the same to my father; he doesn't care. I think my parents only got married because of my maternal grandfather, who didn't like the idea of them moving to Málaga without being married.

But one day I would like to get married; I'm not sure when, but one day. And I'd really like to have some children, that's for sure. Despite all the help from the government it's still not good for working women who have children. In the clinic where I work we all get on really well, but now we have one girl who is expecting. She has some health problems and has to take sick leave so now she is worried that she will get the sack. I don't think my boss will dismiss her but by the time she has had the baby she will probably have been off work for almost a year. It won't be the same for her when she returns.

Take me for example: I work forty hours a week, from 9am until 2pm, then from 4pm until 9pm. I have two mornings off a week, but I need them to go to the supermarket and do the shopping. I also have to work sometimes on a Saturday morning. How could I have a child and continue with my job? I'd have to leave it in a nursery or with one of the grandparents. A nursery is very expensive; it would take half my salary, so what's the point. I know my parents wouldn't want a full-time commitment as baby-minders but Carlos's mother might. She's a housewife and has never worked. Besides which she's very young; she had her children when she was young and she would like to be a young grandmother. In fact she can't wait for Carlos or his sister to start a family. But if I have a child I want to enjoy it, not wait until I'm a grandmother. I'm sure looking after children when you're forty isn't the same as when you're in your twenties.

My friends don't think like me; they all want their children as late as possible. Also they don't want to start living with anyone until they are in their thirties. I think Carlos and I have a more European view of life. We have both travelled abroad a lot. Quite often when we are in a group of friends we get on better with the foreigners than with the Spanish. It's just our way of behaving, more independent.

My parents have always been very modern and liberal minded, although they can be very protective as well. From the age of fourteen they sent me abroad to learn English. The first time I stayed with a family and the woman gave me classes; I was quite happy; I didn't mind being away from home. The second time though I missed my friends. My father would say: "I don't mind where you go as long as there are no Spaniards within a hundred kilometres, so you are forced to speak English."'

She laughed and continued:

'Actually my parents wanted me to have as broad an education as possible. Not only did they want me to speak English but they wanted to be sure I spoke Spanish well. My mother is from Madrid and she would not let me speak with a Málaga accent; she insisted I complete the endings of all my words. I must have sounded strange to my friends because I was often asked where I came from.

There are less people going to university these days; they all think what's the point if there's no job when we finish. Another problem I see with young people is that so many of them take drugs; it's amazingly easy to get drugs and they are not expensive. Everybody does it. It's like twenty years ago when you smoked because everyone else in your group was smoking only now it is drugs. You see people as young as fourteen smoking hash and drinking; it is a shame and it doesn't matter if you are from a rich area or a poor one; it seems to be the same. I'm sure a lot of parents don't know what their children get up to.'

'Tell me about your boyfriend. Does he help you with the housework?' I asked.

'Yes, he helps with everything. He's amazing. My area is the kitchen; I prefer to do all the cooking and shopping. I'm a disaster at keeping the flat tidy so Carlos cleans and tidies, although we do have an Ukranian woman, Natasha, who comes in to clean for three hours once a week as well. He also does the washing up. I used to wash all the clothes because Carlos said he couldn't work the old washing machine that was in the flat. Every two weeks he is away in Madrid or Coruña and he comes back with loads of dirty clothes, so I told him we had to buy a new washing machine. Now he knows how to use it so he does his own washing.

We have separate bank accounts; I have my money and he has his. He pays all the bills: electricity, rent, telephone etc. I pay for the food, the cat and the cleaning lady.

I'm glad we have Natasha to help us because I am always so busy; I never have any spare time. My father rang me the other day to ask if I would like to help them paint their house. I said I would love to but I just don't have the time.'

She smiled and added:

'But I'm very happy.'

Women and Employment

In 2002 according to the Spanish National Statistics Institute only 38% of Spanish women were employed compared to 63% of men. In the years from 1980 to 2000 the number of women in work had increased from 3.5m to 4.7m with almost two million more seeking work.

In 2002 there were also 522,700 women in regular employment who were not covered by the National Social Service System. This accounted for 17% of working women. They mostly worked in domestic service jobs, industrial cleaning, hotels, restaurants and shops. Whereas only 3% of employed women were foreigners, it rose to 11% for irregular workers and this figure was even higher amongst domestic workers, 19%.

The Spanish Government have been looking at the question of equal employment opportunities for men and women since 1988, when their first "Plan for the Equality of Opportunities between Men and Women" was introduced. The emphasis was on access to employment, working conditions, reducing female unemployment and sex discrimination. In 1993 the second plan moved its priorities to the protection of women's employment, changing women's image and their promotion to more senior positions. In 1997 the Government formulated a third plan which incorporated measures to combat gender discrimination and to encourage women's participation at all levels of society. Their fourth plan which was produced in 2003, considered broader areas of inequality and addressed items such as quality of life, equality in civil life and the conciliation of work and family.

Although Spanish women's participation in the labour market has risen, it still lags behind many countries. In 2004 the employment rate for women was 47.7% compared to over 55.7% in the rest of Europe and unemployment for the same year was 15.3% compared to 9.8% of European women and 8% of Spanish men. Women in Spain also earned 25% less than men doing similar work.

According to the Women's Institute, many women still have problems reconciling their work with their family life. Childcare leave was requested by 96.3% of working women in 2003 and maternity leave by 98.4%. It is still mostly the mothers who look after the household.

MARGARITA was born in Melilla in 1953

Margarita (Margo) is married with two teenage children. She works as an auxiliary nurse in mental hospital. She was born in Melilla, the daughter of an army officer and moved frequently with her parents. She has lived in Málaga since she married.

I had met Margo many years ago at a birthday party of a mutual friend. She was a plump, dark haired, lively woman who went out of her way to make us welcome. Her husband had lived and worked in England for many years and spoke perfect English, so she had steered him into the seat next to my husband, who at that time still struggled to make himself understood in Spanish. Now she greeted me like an old friend and ushered me through her large, airy house and out onto the back patio. Her two teenage children were at school and her husband was working so there were just the two of us and a rather bouncy dog, whose barks punctuated our conversation with monotonous regularity. We sat in the shade of a giant umbrella and drank tea and ate very sweet cakes while she told me about her life.

'As you probably remember,' she began. 'I am employed by the *Diputación de Málaga* as an auxiliary nurse in a mental hospital. All the staff work a rota system and nowadays the female staff receive the same pay and conditions as the male staff. I work mornings one week and afternoons the next. It is not very hard work; there are two members of staff for every four patients but older members of staff remember the days when there were thirty patients to one room with only one nurse. That was hard work. But of course nowadays the policy is to release patients into the community whenever possible, so there are fewer patients in the hospital anyway. We have all kinds of people in the hospital, mostly those who would find it difficult to survive outside; for example one of my patients is a grown man with the mental age of a two year old.'

She finished pouring out the tea and sat back in her chair.

'So what do you want to know?' she asked.

'Why don't you tell me about your parents and your childhood,' I suggested.

'OK,' she replied. 'Well although my father's family is from Málaga, soon after he was born he moved to Cadiz; he would always say that he felt more *Gaditano* than *Malagueño,* you know. When he grew up he followed the family tradition and became a regular soldier; he went to the military academy and graduated as an officer. Although the military traditions of his family go back a long way, his own father was a lawyer and worked for the tax office and some members of his family were very wealthy landowners and moved in the highest level of society. His great-uncle, for example, owned a lot of land in Málaga, including houses, churches and even a convent; during the war he gave the convent to the nuns with the proviso that it would be returned to the family if the nuns ever left. I think they are still there. He was a very important man and knew government ministers, politicians, officers and many other powerful people. We even have our own family crest: a shield with the sun and a tree.'

Here she stopped and bending down, picked up a scrap book with a drawing of the crest on the front.

'Look, this is the crest,' she said. 'But I'm not too sure of its significance.'

She put it down and continued:

'But unfortunately for the rest of the family he neglected his estate and bit by bit it all disappeared. He married a very rich and very young Cuban woman who was a friend of Alfonso XIII and who entertained counts and ministers. She even had men writing poetry about her. But despite all her money they managed to lose everything through sheer neglect. Well I say everything but about six or seven years ago the newspaper *El Pais* published a list of investments that my great-uncle had made. It was open to surviving relatives to claim their share. We knew some of that money should really go to our side of the family but in the end we didn't have enough information to prove our case so it all went to his widow's family.'

'What about your mother?' I asked her. 'Was she wealthy?'

'No, my mother is from a small village near Cadiz and is from a very poor family. She met my father when he was stationed in her village and they fell in love and married. She is a clever woman although she didn't receive much education and she has the sweetest nature. My parents had three children: two girls and a boy; I'm the youngest. We were all born in different cities due to my father's postings at the time: my brother in Puerto de Santa Maria, my sister in Ceuta and me in Melilla. I remember my mother telling me how much she enjoyed being an officer's wife. It was a very different life for her; she had servants to cook the meals, clean the house and look after the children which left her free to spend her days socialising with the other officers' wives. Sometimes my father was posted to the same place as her sister's husband, who was also an officer and my mother loved that. She and her sister were very close and they spent a lot of time together. Then when I was four we moved to Málaga and we began to live in the *Pabellones Militares* in the *Camino de Antequerra*, where my mother and her sister still live today. These apartments belonged to the Army and were allocated to officers and their families. The ordinary soldiers lived in *cuarteles*, barracks, but we never lived in them, we always lived in officers' quarters. Nowadays people can buy the apartments and a few years ago my mother bought hers.

Although my father was in the army during the Franco regime, he was not very right wing; he was more middle-of-the-road. Many of the officers had different political views from Franco but they usually kept them to themselves; by and large these were tolerated unless they were extremely left-wing. One of my great-uncles, who had a brilliant military career, couldn't abide Franco; he would always switch the television off if Franco came on. My father was a regular soldier and had a good career in the army; he was a colonel by the time he retired. He had fought at the front during the Civil War, mostly in the north of Spain, but was never injured. He was still alive when Franco died but by that time he didn't agree with anyone, not the *franquistas* or the democrats. My parents didn't talk much about the war; the only thing my mother ever said was that she hated the Reds. If I think about it now I suppose she probably was on the side of the *Falangists*. Her village was in the Nationalist zone during the war and was hardly touched by the fighting, so her own family hadn't suffered.

I'm too young to remember the war but I do remember that there was not a lot of food about when I was growing up even if you had the money to pay for it, but that doesn't mean that we went hungry. The food we ate was always very simple: soups and stews and sometimes fish; there was not the range that you can buy today. The only time we had smoked ham and a good cheese was at Christmas.

When we began to live in Málaga I was sent to a very good convent school; all the officers' daughters went there and their sons went to either the *Agostino* or the *Maristas*, both church schools. My school was very strict, both in the hours we worked and how we presented our work; we had to treat the nuns with great respect and only speak when we were spoken to. I didn't fit in very well because I was very independent and had a strong character; I didn't like the discipline of the school and I suppose I was a bit rebellious. My friend's father was also very strict and would hit her if she answered back but my father had always been more lenient to me so I was used to speaking my mind at home. When I was fourteen and was studying for my Baccalaureate I said I wouldn't go back to the convent anymore, but my father took no notice of me and went ahead and bought my uniform and the books for the next school year. Well when the first day of term arrived I still refused to go. It was the only time my father punished me; he said that if I wouldn't study I would have to work. He sacked our cleaning lady and made me do the cleaning in her place and then told me I had to do lessons with him in the afternoons as well. I thought this was worse; I was working and studying, so I refused to do anything. My parents were furious; they punished me by not allowing me to leave the house except to go to Mass. I don't think my father knew what to do with me. In the meantime my sister continued going to the convent and eventually passed her Baccalaureate and went to university.

Then one day an aunt of mine visited our house; she was the wife of an officer and lived in Granada with her husband and nine sons. My parents decided to send me to live with them. That was great; with nine boys in the house and me the only girl I was treated like a queen. My uncle was very strict and every evening he would make me and his sons gather around a big blackboard and he would give us extra lessons. After a while I began to realise that all my friends were studying and my cousins were studying and their friends were studying and there was only me who wasn't studying. So I returned to Málaga and went to the *Instituto* to study. But it wasn't a lot of good; I tried various courses but didn't finish anything. I even went to a private school to study to be an airline stewardess but soon gave it up. I suppose I was just lazy and didn't want to study.

My father never put any pressure on me to marry, or on my sister. We were not brought up like my mother to learn to cook and sew and embroider things for our wedding trousseau. Besides which we had always had servants so I had never had to do anything; I never even used to make my own bed. I learnt how to do all that when I married my husband; then I would go to see my mother and ask her for recipes so that I could cook a meal for us. I was about thirty by then.

I met my husband when I was on holiday in Vigo, in Galicia, with a friend. He was standing in a bar and I, rather cheekily, asked him where one could go to enjoy oneself. That's how it started. Although he was Spanish he worked in London and even after we were married he continued to work there, coming home at weekends and during the holidays. We were married in church, not because we are religious but because it would please my parents. Then when my first child was born I started working as an auxiliary nurse in the hospital. There were lots more women working by then; you noticed the difference in working conditions for women as soon as Franco died. I've always had firm ideas that everyone has the right to live well; I haven't got much time for all these divisions of class although I must admit you see less differences between the classes nowadays. I think if you study hard and get a good job you deserve it.'

I asked her if she saw much difference between her own teenage years and those of her children.

'Not really,' she replied. 'My daughter knows a lot more about sex and drugs than I did at her age, and she started going out with boys when she was younger. I think youngsters have less respect for their parents and older people generally nowadays. I could always speak openly to my father but I still had great respect for him. As for entertainment, it is much the same today as in my day: I went out a lot with friends to eat and drink, we went to discos and we stayed out until three or four in the morning. Maybe they come home a bit later these days,' she added.

The Military

Until compulsory military service was abolished in 2001 by the conservative government, all young men were expected to serve nine months military or "alternative" service. Increasingly the majority of young men chose the "alternative" service, a form of community work, rather than serve in the armed forces. Conscientious objectors to the military system faced prison or eighteen months "alternative" service. Once conscription ended the army had to turn to a policy of recruitment and this was found to be particularly successful with young women.

Since 1988, following the principle in the Spanish Constitution that all Spaniards were equal, women had begun to apply to join the armed forces. At first they were only allowed to serve as officers in a limited number of corps and services and it was not for another four years that they could serve as soldiers and sailors. In 1999 the Law on Military Personnel allowed them to serve in unrestricted posts, including combat. No segregated units were set up and no limit was set regarding the numbers of women in any one unit.

Today there are more women in the army in Spain than in any other European country. By 2006 there were 14,300 women in the army, 13½% of the force. The career professional today has equal opportunities and rights, regardless of sex; they perform the same tasks, have the same responsibilities, receive the same pay and have to accept the same discipline.

However a number of special regulations have been written to accommodate women members of the armed forces in areas of maternity healthcare, accommodation and uniform. For example if a woman is pregnant at the time she is due to undergo a selection process, she may postpone certain physical tests during this period and take them at a later date. Paternity leave is available for up to sixteen weeks on full pay and they are able to take up to three years unpaid leave for childcare if they so wish. More recently, the creation of nurseries or crèches in military establishments has been agreed to help stabilise the family lives of the personnel. Most military accommodation, except when on field training exercise, is separate for men and women and on older posts has had to be adapted to suit female requirements.

Although women and men are recruited under the same criteria, physical differences between the sexes are allowed, except where it is vital to that particular role. Women wishing to join special operation units, parachutists, divers etc., where physical fitness is paramount, must fulfil the same criteria as men. There has been an attempt to ensure that there are women representatives at all level of the military hierarchy and in each category, including, where appropriate, on military tribunals.

In June 2008 a female cadet graduated top of her class as a fighter pilot.

The admission of women into the armed forces led to a resolution of 18th March 1988 by the Guardia Civil which declared that it could no longer discriminate between the sexes in its selection process and women were to be admitted to its ranks. By 2006 women were working mostly in the areas of civil protection, administration, accounting, legal departments and information, a total of 3.78% of the force.

MARCIA was born in Montijo in 1964

Marcia was born in Montijo, in Extramadura where she still lives with her mother. She is unmarried and has one sister, two brothers and numerous nieces and nephews. She works for the regional government as a pharmacist and spends her free time clay pigeon shooting.

Marcia had arrived to spend a week of her holidays with her sister and brother-in-law. I met her at a party and persuaded her to talk to me about her life. She gave me a bemused smile and agreed to see me later in the week.

We sat on the terrace of her sister's house, in the shade of a large green umbrella and she began to tell me about herself:

'Well, there's not a lot to tell; I was born in 1964 in Extramadura. I have a sister, who you know and two brothers; I am the third, my brother Rafa is the youngest. We were quite a small family, both my mother was an only child and my father had only one sister. We all grew up in Montijo, a small town of only 15,000 people. It was a pretty peaceful place, I was always able to move around with no problems, no danger. I could go to the main square with my friends and my parents never worried.

I went to the local school; it was a mixed school throughout primary and secondary. My elder brother and sister were both sent to single-sex, boarding schools in Badajoz, but when it came to my turn, my mother said no. She told my father that there was no point in having children if they were going to send them away to school as soon as they were nine years old. She wanted to enjoy having them at home. So my father gave in and allowed Rafa and me to go the local school. It was a good school; the girls and the boys were in the same class and we all did the same subjects.

When I was studying for my Baccalaureate at first I didn't know whether to specialise in economics or pharmacy. In the end I decided to become a pharmacist, but it wasn't really a strong vocational choice. At the moment I work for the regional government in the administrative side of pharmacy, but before that I used to work in a high street pharmacy, first of all in Montijo, then in Granada. I enjoy my present job; it's a lot more varied: I work for the *Servicio Extrameña de Salud* in a health centre. It's good. Sometimes I think about having my own pharmacy, but I'm not really sure about it.

In my mother's time women mostly stayed at home; some worked as nurses or teachers, but mostly they looked after their families. Women didn't have much freedom then; there was little opportunity to work and even less to go to university. My mother never worked, neither did my grandmother, nor any of the women in her family. It was traditional for them to stay at home, but to be honest I don't think my mother ever wanted to work. I however, have always wanted to work. I'm not married and I've never met anyone I wanted to marry, but my parents never pressured me to marry. They encouraged me to study and go to university. Things have changed a lot since I was born; for example before 1964 a woman could not have a bank account in her own name, it had to be in the name of her husband or her father. That's all changed now: women have many more rights and many more opportunities. Today women can go into any field of work they want. They drive buses, work in the police force; there are even women astronauts. It's true there are still jobs that are predominantly staffed by women: teaching, nursing and of course pharmacy, but that's their preference. When men and women work in the same job I don't think there's much difference, if any, between their pay, and there isn't really any prejudice against women working, particularly amongst university graduates. I know that more men reach the top of the scale in all jobs; I can see that for myself, in pharmacy, but a lot of the time it's because women don't want the extra responsibility; they want to combine their work and a family. Even if they love their work there comes a moment in their lives when they want to have children. I think they could get the promotion if they wanted it.

I had all the same opportunities as my brothers; the only differences were in the house: Juana and I had to tidy our rooms and help in the house and with the cooking, but the boys didn't have to do anything. They didn't even make their beds. Today it seems to be different; lots more men help in the house. But women are stupid, they want their husbands to help them, but they spoil their sons. They don't realise that they will be husbands too one day.

My father was not a very traditional father; he took me everywhere with him and he called me his little secretary. He would take me hunting with him and taught me to shoot and fish. I loved it. I don't go hunting much now since my father died, but I do a lot of clay pigeon shooting. I've just been to the local Shooting Club in Alhaurin,' she added. 'I can't spend a week away and not do some shooting. It's a fascinating sport: they fire the clays from three machines and you never know which machine it will be or whether it will be coming from the right or the left, or high or low. It's very fast and very exciting. There are twenty-five clays and five different shooting stations; after you have fired at a clay you then have to move to the next station before you can fire again. I usually hit twenty-one, which is quite good. I have won a few cups,' she admitted modestly.

Her sister had already told me that she had won a national competition only a few months before.

'I think I'll continue shooting for a few more years, until I get fed up with it, then I might take up golf. My sister plays a lot of golf and she is always encouraging me to play; she loves it.

The other thing I love to do is travel. I never travelled anywhere as a child, only sometimes to the seaside; our family never travelled outside of Spain. Not many people in our village did. Although I do remember quite a lot of people from Montijo that emigrated to Germany to work when I was a child.'

She laughed and added:

'Now they're all coming here to live.'

She drank some of the cold beer her sister had brought out to us and continued:

'None of our family emigrated though. I started travelling in my twenties and I've been all over Europe: France, Belgium, Austria, everywhere and to Turkey and last year I went to China. The first country I ever visited was Ireland; it was wonderful and the people were so friendly. I really enjoy visiting different countries.'

I asked her about the civil war and if she ever thought about it.

'No, not really; it was a long time ago. Even my mother, who was born in 1934 doesn't talk much about the war; it was really something that had interested my grandparents more. Nobody talks about the war these days, well except Zapatero, who wants people to remember their history, because there are few people left who actually remember the war first-hand.

Even when my father talked about the war, he was only repeating what he had heard from his father. I do know that we had both Republicans and Nationalists in Montijo, and sometimes families were split, with one brother fighting for Franco and the other fighting for the Republic. My childhood wasn't really affected by Franco at all; after all I was eleven when he died and then after that everything began to change very quickly.

Women in business

By 2006 the Chief Executive Officers of Spain's IBM, Microsoft and Google operations were all women. But Spanish women still make up just 4.1% of corporate boards. There are far fewer women than men working in business; this is partly due to the difficulty of combining the task of bringing up a family with a working day that begins at nine o'clock, has a two or three hour lunch break and doesn't end until nine or ten o'clock at night. The CEO at Microsoft, a forty year old mother of three, changed that; she stated that no meetings were to be held in the company before eight thirty in the morning or after five thirty in the evening, a move that has greatly facilitated the working mothers in Microsoft.

Recent research has shown that Spanish boardrooms are very clubby and do not welcome diversity. However the government has recently passed a law stating that by 2015 the boards of all public companies should be made up of at least 40% women. Although there are at present no financial penalties for not conforming to the law, companies could find it harder in the future to get government contracts if they ignore it.

A report in 2007 revealed that in the province of Málaga, over thirty thousand women were employed in jobs well below their qualification level, 12% of working women. There were examples of women with law degrees working as secretaries in offices and a philologist working at the supermarket checkout. According to Chamber of Commerce the situation had deteriorated since the previous year when only 6% were overqualified for the jobs that they did and although the number of working women had increased, seven out of ten jobs did not require qualifications. This was despite the fact that more women were better qualified than men.

EMMA was born in San Sebastian in 1932

Emma was born in San Sebastian, in the Basque country, in the nineteen thirties and currently lives in Madrid. She is the Women's Chairman of the International Golf Federation and was President of the Spanish Golf Federation from 1988 until 2008. She revolutionised golf in Spain: encouraging the building of municipal courses, coaching for children and the formation of successful national teams. She has promoted women's golf all her life.

When I met Emma she had just finished playing in a women's international amateur seniors' competition at Arcos Gardens in the south of Spain. We made our way through the throng of hot, weary and very talkative players on the terrace to look for a quiet corner to sit. Emma seemed to be known by everyone and stopped more than once to enquire how someone had played and if they had liked the course. As we settled ourselves in the corner of the hotel lounge she informed me that she had not played to her handicap of 10.6 that day but did not seem unduly perturbed by it. For a woman of seventy seven her gross 88 seemed pretty good to me. I explained my motives for interviewing her and we began.

'Well of course the world has changed radically since I was young. I know that there are still countries in the world where women are not valued but then there are others where they have very important jobs; women bring very different attitudes to politics and business. By and large women are now participating in all sorts of activities and I think this is good because it can only benefit mankind.

I was born in San Sebastian and so was my mother but my father was from Madrid. He was a diplomat and almost as soon as I was born we moved to Ecuador to live; I lived there for twenty years. When he had the time my father played golf at a course which was very close to the embassy. At first I was more interested in playing tennis but you always needed a partner to play tennis so when I was about seventeen I started playing golf. I found it to be a much more fulfilling game than tennis; there were more variables to consider and it was very technical. Also with tennis you have a limited playing career whereas with golf you can play virtually all your life. After a while I began to play with some of the Americans from the nearby American base. Then when we moved back to Spain I began to play competitively and enter international competitions; that's how my passion for golf began.'

Emma was a member of the Spanish Women's team and went to the Women's World Amateur Team Championship on six occasions; she was captain of the Spanish team when they won the Espirito Santo Trophy in 1986. She has also been Spanish Amateur Champion on five occasions.

'During the time my parents were in Ecuador they sent me to a boarding school in France; they said: "The only thing we can leave our children is a good education". In those days there was not a lot of money to go round but they thought their children's education was very important. Society was very different then, more austere; even though we had a maid, a chauffeur and other servants we never spent money just for the sake of spending it. When I finished school I returned to Madrid to go to university. I wanted to become a diplomat like my father but at that time, in 1956, women were not allowed to be part of the diplomatic service. I spoke quite a few languages so I became an interpreter instead. I was not allowed to go out like you can now and if I went out it was with my fiancé and I had to be home by ten or eleven not three or four in the morning as they do today. For women life was much more controlled. Nowadays it is the opposite; there is a total lack of control; it's chaos. I think young people have lost many values; they have no respect for their parents. I would never have been allowed to speak to my parents they way they do today.

Anyway then I got married; my husband had a job in Madrid so we lived there. I was lucky that my husband played golf too and he allowed me to develop my interest in the game. His mother was an American and so he grew up with a different attitude towards women, not typically Spanish. I would not have put up with a husband who stopped me doing things and kept me at home all the time. We never had any children; if we had had I would never have played so much golf and never become President of the Federation.'

She paused and smiled.

'It will be our Golden Wedding anniversary soon. Of course we argue about things from time to time; that's normal. But it's not like these days, the first argument with your husband and you're off, out the door.

My parents had a house in Andalusia, on the golf course at Sotogrande and we used to go there quite frequently to play golf. I suppose it was in the mid sixties that I became involved in the administrative side of the game as well as playing. Because I spoke a number of foreign languages they wanted me to help them organise the first World Cup in Spain; it was held in 1965 at the *Club del Campo* in Málaga. Very close to Sotogrande was a course called La Cañada; it was the first public course in Spain and they encouraged all kinds of people to play, but especially children. I was very keen to get girls to play golf so in 1969 I formed the first international girls' team at junior level. I remember they played very badly in their first international competition but then later those very same girls went on to win the European Cup and a major competition in France.

I was invited to join the Executive Committee at Sotogrande and then in 1979 I was appointed the president of the golf club. The late seventies and eighties were very bad years for Spain and as nobody wanted to take over the presidency at Sotogrande I stayed on until 1989. But by then I was becoming more and more involved with the Spanish Golf Federation; I knew lots of people in the golfing world and once again because of my proficiency with languages I was asked to help. It was a difficult time for the Spanish Federation whilst the government was trying to establish the new Regional Autonomies. Then in 1988 I was asked to become President of the Royal Golf Federation of Spain (RFEG). The RFEG is responsible for all aspects of golf within Spain: amateur, professional, men, women and children. There are eighteen autonomous golf federations, one for each of the country's regional autonomies and they control all the competitions, handicaps and courses but the RFEG has the overall responsibility. It was a great honour to be invited to be the president. There was no resistance to a woman becoming president but of course in those days a woman had to use a lot more force to achieve anything than a man in the same situation. I believe I have the respect of both men and women although I have met some difficult people from time to time but then that always happens.

When I became President I realised that one of my first tasks was to organise the national teams; to get Spain recognised as an international competitor. In this respect I think we have been very successful. I also wanted to push the women golfers on; at first there was some resistance to this from my male colleagues but that soon disappeared, partly because the women amateur players were much better than the men and had more success. The women's team won two World Cup matches and many European matches. Nevertheless I suppose I have been fighting for women's golf now for forty-three years.

My other great passion was to develop the sport of golf to a popular level by encouraging the building of more public courses and junior golf. I want golf to become a very popular sport, enjoyed by everyone so I give as much support as I can to junior golf; I am pleased to see all the good work that courses such as La Cañada do to encourage the juniors and organisations such as the First Tee Foundation. I am also very proud of the new National Centre of the Royal Spanish Golf Federation that was built in 2005; it is unlike anything else in Europe. The centre and its golf course are fully integrated into the city of Madrid, with public access by metro and bus. It is open to the public and very popular.

I was the chairman of the 1997 Ryder Cup National Committee when the match was held at Valderama in Spain. That was a very exciting time and of course as I'm sure you remember we won by 14 ½ to 13 ½.

Sometimes I look back and think maybe I have missed some opportunities in my life; not the least of which is an economic one because the Federation does not pay me. It was all voluntary work. Occasionally I feel a bit disappointed but then when I look back at what I have achieved and all the honours I have been awarded I think well I must have done something right. In 1998 I received the Gold Medal of Merit in Sports and then King Juan Carlos presented me with The Royal Order of Isabel La Catolica. (Do you know that my father received the first title that our king ever bestowed on anyone). Then in 2001 I was the first women to receive the Christer Lindberg Bowl for global contribution to golf from the European Professional Golfers' Association. All my awards have been for my contributions to golf and my work for women's golf. But the awards don't matter to me; what's important to me is if I did something well or badly. Of course it's satisfying to have world respect but I didn't get involved in any of this for the recognition; it was because of my passion for the game. I have been lucky I have had very loyal and experienced teams and I have been successful. I suppose it has a lot to do with my character; if I see a clear solution to something I just go for it; if something is evidently just then I will not be moved. I suppose I am a bit *machista* in that respect but I am always consistent. Women are capable of doing many things but it has always been much more difficult for a woman to achieve things here because Spain has always been a very *macho* country. If a man makes a mistake, well so what; if a woman makes a mistake everything becomes so much more difficult. I retired from the presidency last year after twenty years service and now have the title of Honorary President. But I am not finished with golf yet; I am still the Women's Chairman of the International Golf Federation. The IGF was founded in 1958 to encourage the international development of the game and to foster friendship between people; it is active in more than a hundred countries. I will remain as the Women's Chairman until 2012. And last year I was part of the committee that selected Rafael Nadal, the tennis player for the 2008 Prince of Asturias Award for Sports. I am also an honorary member of the annual International Conference on Golf and the Environment. So I still have plenty to do. I think golf has many benefits for the community: economic, social and environmental. It has been my passion for many years.'

Women in government

Since 1979 the number of women representatives in parliament has increased considerably; in the 1993-1996 legislature 15.7% of the Congress of Representatives were women and 12.5% of the Senate, and in 1994 they held 12.9% of senior positions in the government. From then on it was full steam ahead. In 2004 a woman was elected as the Vice President of the Congress of Deputies and in July 2007 the new housing minister was a woman. The "40%" rule introduced in 2006 prohibited one sex from taking more than 60% of the candidates in any one political party. But the greatest changes came about because the Socialist Prime Minister, Jose Luis Rodriguez Zapatero vowed to make gender equality a hallmark of his second term of office. In 2008 his new cabinet contained more women than men, nine to eight; there were women ministers of science and innovation, transport and development, education, social affairs and sport, public administration, housing, agriculture and the environment and the Deputy Prime Minister was also a woman. But the appointment that caused the older men to lament and moan over their morning aperitif in bars across the country, was the appointment of Carmen Chacon, a constitutional law professor, as the first female Defence Minister at a time when she was seven months pregnant. What clearer signal could be sent out to the women of Spain that from now on they could be mothers, career women or both; the choice was theirs. Not everyone was happy with the announcement however and the conservative daily newspaper, "El Mundo" published a furious editorial that called it "an exercise in political marketing", claiming that it offended both the traditional values and culture of the army.

However at a time when women undergraduates outnumbered men it seemed to make sense.

MARIA INMACULADA was born in Málaga in 1968

Maria lives at home with her mother and younger brother. She was born in Málaga, but travels all over Spain in her work as golf administrator for the Professional Golf Association. When she was younger she was a member of the Spanish Ladies Golf Team and played golf in many countries. She is unmarried.

Maria is a tall, athletic looking woman, with clear skin, deep brown eyes and shiny, black hair, cut short. The delicate bones of her face give her a typical Spanish beauty. With some reluctance she agreed to meet me for a coffee and talk about her life.

'My life isn't very interesting,' she said. 'I have three sisters and one brother; I'm the fourth child. My three sisters were born in Madrid and still live there and my brother and I were born in Málaga.'

I already knew that she lived in Málaga with her mother and her brother.

'My father died in 1992 of a heart attack. It was unexpected, but he did smoke a lot. It's strange, but after he died, my sister was sorting through his papers to find something about the insurance when she came across a letter he had written the day before he died, saying what he was leaving to each of his children. The writing was really shaky, quite awful in fact. He must have been feeling ill but had said nothing to anyone because he had an important business meeting to go to that day. He was a civil engineer, mainly working on the construction of roads.

I had a wonderful relationship with my father; I think I'm more like him than my mother. At home it was always my mother who punished us, never my father. My father always liked his daughters best; when my brother was born my father was not really that interested in him. Of course that changed later.'

I asked her how she had started playing golf.

'My father was a very keen tennis player but one day he damaged his elbow and couldn't play anymore. Some friends of his used to play golf and he decided to take it up as well. I was only nine at the time but I was fascinated by his golf clubs and I used to go with him to the golf course, carrying his clubs and acting as his caddy.

Then one summer he took all the family to Torrequebrada Golf Course to have some golf lessons with the professional Juan Jimenez, the brother of Miguel Angel Jimenez. I loved it but my brother and my sisters were not so keen. For a while we all played, but now I'm the only one who still plays. My mother still plays a bit, but not as much as she used to.

My sisters went back to Madrid to study and then continued to live there, but I studied Tourism here in Málaga. I suppose all my life I have been involved in the world of golf. I started playing in competitions, then by the time I was fourteen years old my handicap had gone down to sixteen and I was picked for the girls' team. Nowadays with that handicap you would not get a look in; you'd have no chance. My parents were pleased that I played and that I did well but they never became involved; it was my thing. I had to get myself around without any help from them. They never took me to any matches or came to support me and I never expected it. I remember once going to a competition at the Parador Golf Club on my Vespino, with my bag of golf clubs over my shoulder. You couldn't do that now; the police would stop you. Nowadays parents take their children everywhere, but not then. My father worked hard and had five children; he needed some time for himself, he couldn't spend all his free time ferrying us around. Anyway it made me more independent and I learned to value things more.

Things were different then; I remember that when I started playing for the Andalusian team, I had a handicap of eight and it was like being a star. Nowadays the national team has twenty players with handicaps of zero and the worst handicap is four. They have team psychologists and personal trainers; they work out in the gym as well as practice their golf.

Even when I was no longer playing in the team I was on quite a few committees for women's golf: the Andalusian and the Spanish. When I was twenty-four I became the captain of the Spanish children's golf team. That was fun, but a lot of responsibility. I remember I had to take the team of six children to the British Open. For the first time in my life I had to drive a mini-bus and not only that, but on the right hand side of the road.'

She laughed at the memory, her teeth flashing white against her tanned face.

'And on top of that I was responsible for everything, their luggage, the money and the children, themselves, children, well more like teenagers, up to eighteen years old.

If I wasn't playing golf I was running golf competitions; always something to do with golf. I began to work in the golf shop here for a while then I became the manager. That lasted about three years then I got this job with the PGA. I love it. It means travelling all round Spain organising professional golf competitions.'

Maria (on the left) with her team

'Yes, I saw you on TV once,' I said.

'I heard about that from some friends; I think it must have been at La Cala. I do enjoy the work but soon I need to look for something more permanent. The trouble with this job is that there is no work in the winter for at least three months because there are no competitions then. I think I'll try to get a job in a hotel with a golf course; then I'll be able to use my Tourism qualifications and my golf experience. It would be nice to have a fixed contract and better social security cover.'

'Tell me something about your charity work,' I suggested.

'Well I have always liked to help the needy in whatever way I could. A few years ago I went to Burkino Faso in West Africa with my friend Lucia to see if there was any way we could help the children there. We planned to organise a golf competition to raise money to buy them books and clothes. It's one of the poorest countries in Africa, you know. Lucia, who's a dentist, had already heard of it because whenever they replace old dental equipment or furniture they send the old stuff out there. Burkino Faso was quite an eye-opener for me. We were only there fifteen days but it was very sad to see such poverty.

Then my friend Teri asked me if I would help with the "*Nuevo Futuro*" charity. It's a national charity run entirely by women, with Princess Pilar as their president; they raise money to support children who have no-one to care for them, whose parents are either in prison or are drug addicts. The charity owns a number of flats throughout Spain; between six and eight children live together in these flats with a *monitor*, house-mother, to look after them. Each flat requires three *monitores* to give a twenty-four hour cover and they all have to be paid, so it's pretty expensive. The *monitores* do the shopping, take the children to school or to the doctor when necessary and generally look after them. The charity has to pay for school books, clothes, food and anything else the children need. The children can stay in these flats until they are eighteen years old then sometimes they take over jobs as *monitores* so that they can stay on.

There's quite a lot of work to do; in Málaga we have forty or fifty flats, all bought by "*Nuevo Futuro*". The local council helps as well; they often sell us cheap flats and they match all the money we raise. For example each December we hold a "*rastrillo*", a Christmas market in the *Palacio de Congresos* in Málaga; it is our main fund raising event of the year and lasts five days. We have a big stall selling all sorts of produce for Christmas: hams, smoked meats and sausages, wines, nuts, cheese, gifts. Everything is donated so we make a hundred percent profit on everything and all the money raised goes to the charity and the local council donates an equivalent amount. We also sell space to shops who want to have a Christmas stall there; they pay a fixed amount according to the size of their stall and they usually donate things for us to sell as well. Then there is an entry fee of one euro for everyone who comes to the *rastrillo*.

I have been working with "*Nuevo Futuro*" now for about five years. We meet every week in a house owned by the charity. Although it's not a religious organisation, most of the women who run it are very religious and quite old. It makes me a bit sad because it seems to me that it's past its sell-by-date. By that I mean that 90% of the women are of an older generation, who have never worked and always had plenty of free time to devote to charity work. Now they are getting older and there's no-one to take their place. Their daughters all go to work and don't have the time. Our boss is seventy now and she's talking of giving it up. She'd like me to take over from her but I've said no. I said I'd help her as much as I could but that she should continue; after all she's the one with all the experience and contacts. She knows all the people who sponsor us and donate things for us to sell. Maybe in about ten years I'll take over from her, but not now.'

She paused to take a drink of lemonade then decided to tell me some more about her family:

'I'm not really religious. The only one in my family that's religious is my mother; she goes to Mass every week. It's funny though, my sisters never went to church but now that they have children they have started to go again so that their children can get confirmed.

We're a pretty united family despite the fact that some of us are in Madrid and some in Málaga. I didn't know my grandparents; my grandfather was killed during the Civil War. He was taken from his home in Madrid and shot by the Republicans for no real reason except being a Nationalist. My grandmother was pregnant with her third child at the time. She had to bring up three children with no husband, so she sold her family land to support them. After the war the government offered her a pension, but she refused it, saying that there were people who needed it more than her.

My other grandfather was also a Nationalist, but he was a doctor. When they came to shoot him he told them that he was neutral; he would treat anyone who needed his services. As they were very short of doctors by then they let him live. He and his wife lived in Almansa and they had three children too. My grandfather never had much money because nobody had any money to pay him; he was paid with whatever people could afford: a chicken, some eggs, a cheese, some potatoes. My grandparents were never rich but they were never short of food.

My parents met in Madrid and got married. After a few years my father went looking for work; he wanted to live by the sea, either in Valencia or Málaga. It turned out to be Málaga.

I talk to my sisters every day and go to Madrid to see them as often as I can. One of my sisters has three girls; the first two were twins but they were born prematurely at six and a half months and one suffered severe brain damage. They spent three months in an incubator before the doctors realised that there was something wrong with one of them. I used to go a lot to help my sister and I remember one of the babies vomiting all the time. We said this can't be right, one baby OK and the other being sick all the time. So we talked to the doctors and they agreed to do some tests on her and then found that she had suffered some brain damage through lack of oxygen when she was being born. It's sad; the damage has affected her muscles and she cannot walk or use her hands to lift anything, not even to wipe her nose; if you put her on the sofa she has to stay there. She spends her time in a wheelchair and has to be lifted into the bath or into bed. She is getting quite heavy now because she is a healthy girl; there is nothing wrong with her internal organs, only her muscles. Her mind is also fine but she has difficulty talking because she can't move her tongue; the tongue is a muscle too. I can understand what she says because I am used to her now and I love her very much; besides being my niece she is also my god-daughter and she's called Maria after me.'

She pulled out her wallet and showed me a picture of three dark-haired little

girls, two of them in white dresses with flowers in their hair.

'That's Maria and her sisters. When her twin-sister took her communion three years ago they wouldn't allow Maria. But this year she took it with her younger sister even though she is now eleven. It was the priest's suggestion. I think it was very nice of him because many priests won't let children with disabilities take the communion because they say they don't understand what they are doing. I wasn't able to go to the communion because I had to work so Maria was very upset; my sister said she cried for half an hour.

It's hard work for my sister; she has a girl that lives-in to help her with Maria, but it's not the same as family so I like to go and help her whenever I can. They have become like my own children, because I spend such a lot of time with them. Of course I love my other nephews and nieces as well but these ones are special.'

Women's Golf

When the President of the Royal Spanish Federation of Golf, Emma Villacieros retired in 2008 her successor, Gonzaga Escauriaza said that she would be remembered for the spectacular increase in the number of golf federations, the growth in the number of public golf courses in Spain, for putting Spanish golf on both the European and world maps and for her contribution to the development of women's golf. In the years 1988 to 2004 there was an increase in federated members from 50,000 to 258,000 and the number of course increased from 90 to 266.

Thanks to the support of the Spanish Federation the women's amateur team has grown from strength to strength. Four young Spanish women have won the prestigious Ladies' British Amateur Open in the last eight years; in 2001 Marta Prieto became the first Spaniard ever to win it then in 2003 it was won by Elisa Serramia. In 2006 the eighteen year old Belen Mozo from Cadiz won both the British Ladies' Amateur and the British Girls' Amateur Opens. The seventeen year old Carlota Ciganda played in the Junior Ryder Cup in 2006 and in 2007 won the Ladies' British Amateur. The strength of the current team is reflected in the fact that the Spanish Ladies' Amateur team was seeded second when it went to the European Women's Amateur Team Golf Championship in Sweden in 2008.

SARAH was born in Venezuela in 1949

Sarah (usually known as Sally) was born in Venezuela but moved to England when she was still a baby, where she lived until 1994 when she and her husband decided to move to Spain. She is married with two grown-up children. She trained to be an artist and now divides her time between helping her husband run their holiday accommodation and painting.

It was only a week before Christmas but the sun had been shining all day so Sally suggested we sit outside on the terrace. She was a small, trim woman with light brown hair and a sparkling face that belied her age; she looked more like a forty year old than someone fast approaching sixty. I asked her to begin by telling me something of her background.

'Well I was actually born in Venezuela. My father worked for Shell and had already been there some years when I arrived but he was transferred back to England when I was only eleven months old. I had to have a Venezuelan passport even though my mother insisted I was British.'

At this point she stopped and giggled.

'I was only six weeks old, so it read: "Height 18 inches, Hair blonde, Eyes Blue." It was written in the most beautiful copperplate writing. Anyway when I became eighteen I had to choose my nationality and naturally I chose British. It's a shame I didn't live longer in Venezuela because I would have learnt Spanish, which would be very useful now. My father spoke good Spanish but he never taught me.

Neither of my parents was artistic; they played golf,' she declared with an emphasis that spoke of her low regard for the game. 'But my grandparents and both my brothers paint. I don't know if it's in the genes; I suppose it depends whether you believe talent is learnt or hereditary. An artist friend of mine believes it is learnt but I think you must have a leaning for it first. I'm sure if I'd been born into a family where they all loved numbers I would have left early.

Anyway I grew up in England and went to art school. It was never anything unusual for me; I was always drawing long before that. I think my parents used it as a way to keep me quiet, "Sit there and draw that," they would often tell me. I have friends who think of art as quite revolutionary and I just can't understand why they find it so strange. For me it has always been a way of life.

In actual fact I didn't get on all that well at art school. I think the idea of an art school is a bit suspect anyway; the old method was to be apprenticed to a master and learn from him how to mix the paints and prepare the canvas. Nowadays they have a particular way of teaching that is very prescriptive, "This is the way and this is how you should paint." Also I find the tutors rather lazy; they only see the pupils for tutorials once or twice a term and the rest of the time they're on their own. It's no wonder they exhibit piles of tyres in the Tate Gallery as works of art.

Living in Spain is much better for my art; the light is better, the colours, the contrasts of light and shade. You haven't got the endless grey days with no light that you have in England. Also the Spanish have a more open attitude to art; galleries and restaurants are more prepared to display your work without you being famous first. In England you have to be famous before anyone will put your art up and you can't become famous because no-one will display your work. Here they're much more encouraging. I wonder if it's something to do with Franco and the fact that he squashed the arts and now they are slightly better received. It's like they are catching up on everything. I think it's a very vigorous feeling here because they are grasping the new; they're excited about new things, new possibilities. In the art world they are very open-minded. My own art is rather old fashioned but the Spanish like abstract and modern art.

I think Spain's a very positive place to live, a bit like England in the sixties. There you had the generation born after the war, growing up in the sixties and wanting to grab hold of everything, saying "We're here now and it's going to be different." Maybe every generation feels like that but I think that it was a sixties' thing to say anything is possible. That's what's happening here in Spain now.

Another marvellous thing is that you find art everywhere. You can go into a chemist shop, like the one here in Benajarafe where they have an enormous painting by Robert Harvey on the wall. You go in there and it just hits you in the eyes, a landscape of hills, trees, grasses and sky. I think, yes why shouldn't you have art in the chemists.

They are also very good at encouraging the children in schools to participate. Local artists, both Spanish and foreigners go in and work with them and at the school in Benagalbon they have regular exhibitions of artists' work. When we take our painting holiday students up to the village to paint people come out from their houses and ask if we need water for our paints. They always show lots of interest in what we're doing.'

At this point we were interrupted by her husband who wanted to tell her he was going up to check on the land. Their *finca* is surrounded by forty thousand square metres of mango trees which he cultivates with the help of a local man. After exchanging a few pleasantries we resumed our conversation and soon could hear the rumble of his tractor going up the hill.

'Artists are a funny lot you know,' she added. 'They are very competitive. If you show a fellow artist your work he is very reticent to offer any praise. All you'll get is "Hmm" and he'll change the subject.

Spanish artists are less snobbish about their work. When Robert Harvey was alive he had a group of artists who met regularly at his home in Macharaviaya. Some were very well known, like Fernando de la Rosa, an abstract artist and Robert himself. But there was one, Paco, who lived in Los Puertas and was basically a bricklayer. He painted at night, in his garage under a fluorescent light. They are what you would call "naive" paintings and are absolutely charming. He's accepted as part of the group on the same level as everyone else despite the fact he's not what you would call a "proper" artist. You don't have to go to art school to be an artist here.

Spanish women seem to do more craft work than painting. It's probably something to do with the fact that painting is a solitary occupation whereas craft work is usually done in groups. I used to go to a stitch-work class and there were women of different nationalities there. What was so fascinating was that each nationality had a different style to their stitching; the Danish style was very different from the English and both were different to the Spanish. I'm going to join a women's craft group in Benajarafe next month; they meet every Tuesday and Thursday in one of the rooms next to the post office.'

I asked her why they had decided to make their home in Spain.

'Well Denis's parents had a house here and we used to come to visit them. I remember the first time we came here, we left London in a snowstorm and arrived to blue skies; we walked on the beach, we played tennis and we relaxed in the warmth. I thought this is stunning and there and then we decided to look for our own place. We've been here fourteen years now and I feel very much at home. When I first came I used to write down anything that I thought was quaint or strange or funny, then after about two years I stopped. Then when I went back to England I was hit by how quaint and strange and funny things were there so I began to write those down instead. I don't think I would like to go back to England; life seems very constricted and narrow there now. Too many cameras. I like the way the Spanish have this slightly rebellious attitude to authority. Obviously one doesn't want to go right off the other end and become an anarchist but I think a healthy independence is good.'

She then went on to explain to me that they had four houses set in a quadrangle which they let to tourists. This holiday complex had its own swimming pool and tennis court and the guests could also wander around the grounds if they wished. In the low season they ran fully catered painting holidays and hired local artists to give the classes.

'You really have to make your money in the summer to keep you going through the winter; it's the same for the whole tourist industry. I'm very lucky because the lettings and the painting holidays allow me to paint what I like. It may sound a bit decadent but it is actually a great luxury for an artist to be able to do exactly what they choose.

There's a great deal of work for both of us when the painting holidays are on. We organise everything for them: trips to interesting places, meals, entertainment. We have a cook that comes in during the week but Denis and I do the meals at the weekends and I usually make the puddings. I love eating puddings and normally forbid myself them but this is a good excuse.

I like having new people around and getting to know them. You get to see different aspects of people's nature. They're usually English people but occasionally we have some Spanish.'

I asked her if there had been any problems with integrating into Spanish society.

'All the people who work here, the gardener, the lady who does the changeovers in the houses, the cook, they are all Spanish so it is very important that we can speak the language. When we first arrived we went to Spanish classes and we still keep going back from time to time to improve. Denis of course, having the mango farm, meets lots of the local farmers and is very much in touch with what's going on. He's just been invited to join the village festival committee and is really enjoying it. The Spanish love their festivals and there are quite a number during the year. It's just up Denis's street. I'm not too involved in that except when he wants me to make mince pies or something. It's easier for him to mix with the local people than me; he can go to the local bar and have a beer and talk about football to the men. It's more difficult for me to meet new people because Spanish ladies tend to spend more time in their homes. I go to a yoga class and Pilates, both of which are run by Spanish women. Then we have a few Spanish friends who invite us to eat out with them and Mari, our neighbour invites us to the pig-killing every year. Now that's an interesting event.

I have to admit that after the last one we're not actually very keen to go again, even though we don't go when they are killing the pigs. They get a *matador* chappie who comes in and kills them. It's quite interesting; the vet comes the night before and makes sure they're clean and fit for eating then a professional *matador* comes along the next day and kills them. The family spend all day preparing them.

We walked over there quite early. It was really surreal because they had two pigs and they cut them down the middle and hung them up in the trees; there were the head, legs and body slung over trees while the family were preparing the other bits: making the *morcilla*, black pudding and sausages, cutting up the chops. It just looked like a Salvador Dali painting, you know, "The Melting Watches". When it's all prepared they have a big barbecue. They use the whole pig; nothing is wasted. It's very interesting; we've been to quite a few now. It's usually just the family, which is rather large given all the nieces and nephews and us. Last time Denis went rather green; he said it was the smell of the blood. I have to admit I didn't notice it; I've got no sense of smell so it didn't put me off.

We get involved in other local events as well. There's the Romeria for example, where they bring the saint out of the church in Benajarafe and put her on an ox-cart and drag her up to the church in Benajarafe Alto. The ox-cart is followed by a second cart that is laden with wine and smoked ham. They stop every so often to give the oxen a rest and that is an excuse to eat and drink a little. There's a *verdiales* band that accompanies them so everyone has a bit of a dance too. It makes for a very slow journey.

When they get to the church that's when the fun starts; there's lots of music and games. Many of the young men come on horseback and they participate in a strange competition. A wire is stretched across the road and a number of tape loops are tied to it. The idea is that the horseman rides full tilt at the wire and tries to capture one of the loops on a pencil.

The Romeria

They then attach the loops to their saddles and the one with the most is the winner. I expect years ago they used a spear or a lance rather than a pencil. They have lots of traditional events like that; it's quite fun.

I get lots of inspiration for paintings from these local events. You know there are lots of reasons for painting: some want it to be decorative; some want it to say something about the state of humanity or politics or whatever; I like to record what's going on, the traditions. I suppose it's because I think they will eventually just fade away and because they're interesting.'

It was beginning to get cold by then so Sally suggested we move into the house and sit by the fire.

'I have noticed a lot of changes in the time we've been here,' she resumed. 'Especially amongst young women who quietly, with no fuss and no feminist movement, have gone to university and trained to become lawyers, chemists, doctors, even politicians. And all the young lads must wonder what's hit them. I take my hat off to them; they just got on with it. Another thing I've noticed is the change in the size of families; Mosquito, a friend of our children, is one of a family of ten but I'm sure he will only have one or two children himself. Then there's an old woman I know in the village who had fifteen children. I expect the young people are soon going to start experiencing the sorts of pressure we have in England: mortgages, both partners having to go to work.'

I asked her about her own children, Tom and Louisa.

'Tom works in Paris and Louisa is in London but she travels around the world a lot. She would like to live in Australia. It would be nice if they lived here but I can't see it happening. It wasn't something I thought about before we moved here; I suppose I never really considered it as an option. For a start the pay is appalling and for another it is not easy to break into the social groups. It is difficult for them to make friends when all the local youngsters are already in social groups that were formed when they were at school or university.'

She laughed and added:

'Anyway Louisa is probably too tall for the average Spaniard. It would be nice to have them here though. I know it would be Denis's idea of heaven if they both came home to live and work.'

Women painters

*"The female artist is merely ridiculous,
But I am in favour of female singers and dancers."
Pierre-Auguste Renoir*

Although there is a traditional belief that women artists never really existed, recent studies and exhibitions have proved otherwise. An exhibition in 1976 in Los Angeles, entitled "Women Artists 1550-1950" displayed a range of women artists who spanned those four hundred years. A misconception has always held that "art" is man's work and "craft" a woman's. Removing the line between art and craft changes the picture somewhat. Historically many factors were at work against women artists: the fact that male artists dominated the academies and could restrict the entry of women; that until the 20th century women were not allowed to attend the same art classes as men; that they were not allowed to compete on an equal basis in the competitions and that the genres that women were allowed to paint, such as landscapes and portraits, were of less importance to the critics. Sometimes women artists were accused of letting their husbands do the painting for them so they would often make a point of painting in full view of people to prove otherwise.

Although some women artists are found listed as member of the artists guilds in northern Europe during the 16th century there is no mention of any woman working as an artist or selling art in the annual guild censuses in Valencia, Spain at that time. When the widow Inés Alvarez applied for a licence to take on the work of silversmith on the death of her husband in 1630 she was refused. A hundred years later the records show that the widows of Spanish silversmiths were continuing with their husbands' trade but they were never given licences to do so. A number of women who did work as artists in the 17th century worked for the Royal Court: Luisa Villalobos was a goldsmith, María de Arratia was an embroiderer and Luisa Roldan was an unpaid sculptress.

When the Italian painter Sophonisba Angosciolo of Cremona was invited to Spain by Philip II to paint the portrait of Queen Isabella her official position in the Spanish court was as the Queen's maiden and she worked as a teacher of painting. In Italy Sophonisba already had a well established reputation as a portrait painter but in Spain she was not allowed to sign her work. The king gave her portrait of the Queen to Pope Pius IV as a gift.

Social restrictions also hindered women's ability to become artists. It was considered a great breach of social etiquette for a woman to live in the same house as her maestro, as a young male artist would do. Because of this many women artists came from the families of artists and trained under their fathers or husbands; they could not train with a maestro who was unrelated to them. Not only that but they were unable to enter the academies to learn. In 1901 the Academia de Bellas Artes de España received its first application from a woman for a place at the academy. The Minister of the Exterior sent a telegram asking for clarification on this and received the reply that there was no rule that prohibited it. However there is no evidence that any woman joined the ranks of the academy until decades later, certainly not that particular applicant. Basically women artists were deprived of the chance to learn their craft and kept out of the centres of artistic studies.

A survey done in 2001 on the status of women artists looked at eight European countries: Italy, Austria, Finland, Germany, the Netherlands, Portugal, the UK and Spain. It identified women artists as 38%-45% of all artists, 30%-60% of art students and 3%-20% of lecturers.

Spanish Women Painters

Maria de Abarca *was a distinguished portrait painter who painted in Madrid during the period 1640-1653. She died 1656.*

Maruja Mallo *was born in Lugo in 1902, the fourth of fourteen children. Her father was a customs officer and sent her to Avila to a school of arts and crafts. She began by copying the illustrations that appeared in the magazines of the time. She started exhibiting her paintings in Asturias and when she was twenty she moved to Madrid with her brother to study at the Royal Academy of Fine Art for four years. There she met Salvador Dali and became one of a group of artists known as the Generation of 27, including the poet Federico Lorca and writer and director Luis Buñel. She formed a strong friendship with the philosopher Maria Zambrano and the poet Concha Mendez. She and Concha were the first women to abandon wearing their hats and walk around Madrid at night, unescorted and bareheaded, scandalising everyone. She became equally known for her sculpture as her paintings. When the Civil War broke out she was in Galicia; she stayed there for a few months then slipped into Portugal and left for Argentina. She did not return to Spain until 1964 and by then all her friends were either dead or missing. In 1979 she started her last period of painting at the age of 77. With the death of Franco she gained national recognition and received the Medulla de Oro de Bellas Artes in 1982. She died in 1995.*

Angeles Santos *was born in Girona in 1911, the eldest of eight children. Her father was a civil servant who moved* with his family to Seville when Angeles was a young girl. It was at her boarding school in Seville that she learnt to paint and draw. When the family moved to Valladolid she continued her art studies with a private tutor from Italy and had her first exhibition in 1927 at the age of sixteen. When the Civil War broke out she initially fled to France with her husband but could not bear to be away from her family and returned. She did not rejoin her husband until 1962 when she moved to Paris to live with him. She died in 1999.

Remedios Varo was born in Girona in 1908. She was another painter of the Avant-garde movement of the time. At the start of the Civil War she moved to France where she lived and worked until the Nazi occupation of the city. She fled to Mexico where she lived until her death in 1963 of a heart attack. Her painting style was influenced by the Surrealist movement from her time in Paris and by pre-Columbian art from her years in Mexico. She worked in oil on masonite panels that she prepared herself and her work was considered to have a strong allegorical style.

All three women, Remedios Varo, Maruja Mallo and Àngeles Santos used their paintings to reflect the social changes they saw occurring in Spain, particularly in regard to the growth of feminism.

EVE was born in France in 1944

Eve, whose title is countess, is a member of the Austrian aristocracy. She was born in Vichy France at the end of the Second World War. She is an internationally recognised architect and currently lives and works in the south of Spain.

When I arrived at Eve's house I was shown inside by her Argentine maid, Dora and accompanied by a small dog of unidentifiable origin. The maid seated me in the lounge and busied herself with putting a match to the wood-burning stove that she had obviously cleaned and set earlier. After a few minutes Eve joined me. She was a tall, athletic looking woman, with blonde hair tied back from her face and a beaming smile. After offering me coffee and despatching Dora to make it she settled back on the sofa and began to tell me about herself.

'I am Austrian,' she began. 'Well actually half Austrian; I have dual nationality, French and Austrian. I was born in France at the end of the War. My parents left Austria in the 1930s because life was becoming rather difficult there. They moved to the Caribbean where they had an estate. Our family have had an estate in Santa Lucia for four generations. In 1920 my grandmother lived there as a farmer, growing sugarcane. She owned the domaine Rom Prat and became one of the first women to export rum. She was very innovative with her farming methods and even made rum mixed with exotic fruits. You know it is the only island in the Caribbean where they use elephants on the plantations.'

I must have looked surprised because she laughed and explained:

'You know I think some of my family were probably pirates years ago; people used to lure the boats onto the rocks and then go out under the pretext of helping them but really to help themselves to things from the wreck. Well on one occasion my great, great-uncle went out to the wrecked ship and when they opened the hold there were four elephants there, two males and two females. He took them ashore and bred them. Now today, in 2009 we have their descendants working on the estate.

Well anyway my father, who was a heart surgeon decided to go back to Geneva to work but then the War broke out. He stayed for a while but he was not happy; because he was a doctor he had to vet the men for military service and he began to be unhappy about his role especially as the people he had to pass were getting younger and younger. So he contacted a friend of his who helped him escape to Vichy in France. Unfortunately my father was very outspoken and he would warn people about what was happening and tell them to look out for themselves so the police arrested him and put him in jail. My mother was a very distinctive looking woman and heavily pregnant at the time; she was half Austrian, half Danish. She tried to find my father and she too came to the notice of the French police. They thought she was pretending to be pregnant and hiding something under her dress so they interrogated her and that was when I arrived, on the 9th August 1944. She was lucky because a French butcher that was a member of the Resistance helped her until my father was released. We moved back to the Caribbean and I lived there until the end of the War.'

She laughed again.

'That's what it's like being an aristocrat; you become very good at emigrating. We just take our jewels and we go. So you see I'm used to living abroad; I'm used to being an immigrant.

My father loved France and so when the War ended we moved back to France and I went to school there. He decided when I was born that I should have little or no contact with my mother and I was put with two nurses to look after me. Then when I was three years old I was sent to a boarding school until I was sixteen. So I never really knew my mother. I know she was very beautiful when she was young and she spoke seven languages but she was completely illiterate. It was quite common in those days. I have often wondered how my father could have left her so vulnerable. If anything had happened to him she would have been helpless. As it was she could never relate to me; she was in awe of me. I also sometimes think she was a bit ashamed of me. I used to visit her twice a year but we were never normal with each other; we didn't know each other. Somebody once asked her about me and what I did for a living. She said she didn't know; she thought I designed things.

Later in life she became very ill and when I went to visit her she would not allow me to stay in her house; I had to spend three months in a nearby hotel. She died ten years ago and I went to the funeral. There were only four of us: the maid, two domestic servants and me. One of them asked me who I was.

I believe my mother was a good person. She was happy with her life because she had a lot of money and she could show it off. I suppose I blame my father for her life but that's how it was then.'

Eve broke off to show me an old photograph of her parents and herself at a younger age. Then she continued:

'I love France, especially the south of France because I like the heat. But I am not French; France is not my country. I feel Austrian, especially when I am working. In my private life maybe I am more French, more romantic but in my work I am much more "square". I studied in French and then when I had my diploma in architecture I decided to go to Rome to do a three year specialist course.'

At this point Dora returned with a tray and the coffee. As we helped ourselves to the coffee I asked her how long she had lived in Spain.

'I came here fifteen years ago,' she replied. 'I was married at the time to a high ranking Austrian diplomat. We lived in many different countries and because I was his wife I was not allowed to work. Eventually I decided to stay on in the country to establish myself with some work after he had left then I would join him months later in his new posting. It meant that we were not together very much and although we were good friends it was not a normal life. In the end I told him that it was not working; that neither of us could have a proper life living like that. That was fifteen years ago and I decided if I was not going to live with him I would live somewhere where I felt good. The house in France was too big for me to manage on my own so I decided to sell it and move to Italy. But Italy was too expensive so although I didn't know Spain I decided to come to Spain. At that time I only thought of Spain in terms of package holidays for poor people, sand, sun and sea. Franco had only died in 1975 and people were still a bit afraid; some were staying and some were leaving. I recognised this feeling because my family have often experienced it in the past. So I decided to offer my services as an architect and wait to see what would happen. I thought that Spain, in particular Andalusia was going to improve a lot and I liked the climate. I was not sure that it was going to be right for me socially however.

I received a lot of offers of work, including one in Mojácar in Almeria where they wanted to build a golf course. That area is very special; it is desert and living there is like being at the end of the world. I liked it there; I started to watch and listen and I was happy. The people were so behind compared to the rest of Europe but they had the pretensions to be the best. I worked very hard on my project but I soon found that it was difficult to mix with the people. They had no need of me or my company. I remember one day I went to the local stationery shop to buy a particular type of folder that I had ordered. At that time I had twenty people working for me and we bought all our office supplies from that shop; the woman made a lot of money from us. I asked her about my folder and she said no, she didn't have one. I persisted but she was not interested in serving me. I saw one on the shelf but she still would not get it for me and started to serve someone else. In the end I climbed up and took the folder down myself. This was so typical; they don't care about you and they will be quite rude to you. It's like: "You come here because we have beautiful weather and you stay here and work. We take your money and that's that."

I worked there for a year and then I decided I did not like it there so I began to travel. For the next two years I spent three months in Italy or France and then I would come back to Spain to work. That was until I met my present husband. He's a Canadian, a strong, Indian, mountain man, from Vancouver. He pushed me to see the Spanish countryside with different eyes; he liked the naturalness of the land and the way that the people were happy with what they had. When he came here thirty-seven years ago they were open to everything new; they were not just interested in the money.'

She took a sip of her coffee and then continued:

'Now that's finished. Day by day by day everything has completely changed. They are not educated enough to consider the possibility that being *Andaluz* is better and they have not enough experience so they copy rather than develop their own style and they think that is enough.

My husband is a cowboy, a countryman; he had seven horses. He retired at a young age with plenty of money and he came to Spain to buy land and build. He had never done any building before but he's a practical man and he got on well with the Andalusian country people. He is very different to me but he makes a great companion; we complement each other. So we began to work together on a wonderful dream: to build a Moorish *pueblo.* I know the Andalusians don't like to admit it but they are more Moorish than Spanish. We created seven golf courses and many *pueblos*, all in the style of *Andaluz Moresque.* We used new materials to create an old style, villages with Moorish arches in the reddish Marakesh colour. At first the Spanish did not like it. They said: "Why Arab? We are more Mediterranean, like the French and the Italians, not Arab." I told them no, you are different.'

At this point Eve got up and left the room. She returned a few moments later with a large scrapbook and proceeded to show me photographs and drawings of her projects: villages in Almeria, apartment blocks, hotels and houses, all in what is a well recognised Moorish style. It seemed curious that this style had emanated from an Austrian countess and not from a Spaniard.

'I also do panoramas,' she added pointing to the wooden door that led to the next room. 'Painting on walls.'

The door was painted to look like a bookcase with books on it.

'And this,' she said, beckoning me to follow her.

We went through the door into a conservatory and turned right towards the indoor swimming pool. On the far wall she had painted a full length panorama of beach, sea and palm trees.

'It's called "trompe l'oeil",' she said. 'I have quite a reputation for it now but I actually started doing it because of a mistake I made. I had designed a group of houses set alongside a marina in a small village near St Tropez. The houses were arranged in rows along five spits of land, like five fingers, with water on each side. When they were completed I realised that the very end of each row of houses had a blank wall; it looked awful. When you approached the houses all you saw were five blank walls. There was no time to modify the design because we had a grand opening the following week with a film crew and lots of people, so I got my team together and we painted panoramas on each wall. They looked fabulous and everybody was delighted. After that people began to ask me to paint panoramas for them. I actually learnt the techniques when I was studying in Rome. Do you know that the team I have has been with me for twenty-two years now; all except two are Italians.

At the moment I have the opportunity to design a luxury hotel where every suite in the hotel is different. I like the sound of it but I don't know whether I will do it or not yet. I would like to push the Moorish style of architecture more here in Andalusia but the *Andaluces* have difficulty in accepting it. I think because Franco had no interest in Andalusia the *Andaluces* are not proud of what they have. They have managed to get a reputation around the world that they are robbers. I tell them that they must show that they are now the best and that they have something to offer: their weather, their scenery, their land, their history. If you travel thirty-five minutes towards Algeciras it is more and more African. Soon I think that the *Andaluz* mentality will not exist; it will be taken over by the Arab mentality.

We worked with lots of Spanish people over the years and know lots of them very well but we have never been invited into their homes. I am always inviting people here to things: openings, receptions, birthdays; it is a real pleasure for me to do it. And they love to come; they complement me on the French buffet, the champagne, the art displays, the music, but that's it. They never telephone to thank me afterwards, as the English or the French would do. Sometimes we are invited to a posh restaurant but never to anyone's home. Even today it is the same. We know a surgeon, a notary, lawyers; I have a number of lawyers working for my company including one just for me; I pay him to look after my personal things. He is a very nice man, well educated, very polite; I have known him a long time but even he has never invited me to his home. Instead once or twice a year he takes us to an expensive restaurant. It is the same with the family of my notary; they will not show you their house. It is as if they are ashamed of their own home. They too prefer to take you to an expensive restaurant so that they can pretend to be something more than they are. They have no need of us, only our money.

When we met my husband said we are in Spain so we must speak Spanish; we both speak perfect Spanish. It makes no difference. My husband did a lot for the area around Mojácar; he opened a car-hire company and the first communal swimming pool. The people there adore him because he's a *campasino* just like them, a real countryman, but they still do not invite him to their homes. He had no social life there. He is a bit disillusioned with the Spanish now. I think he was probably rather naive. For him everything was always very clear, black was black and white was white but the Spanish were not like that; what was black one day could be white the next.

When I first arrived in Mojácar they held traditional festivals that celebrated the struggle between the Moors and the Christians. They were wonderful to see. Now it's all finished. Now it's Maseratis and Mercedes.

Do you like the bullfight?' she asked. 'My husband introduced me to bull-fighting. He is a great fan; well being a cowboy he would be. At first it was not my cup of tea but now I say well I am happy to wear leather boots so what's the difference. I suppose it's the spectacle that's difficult for some. But I adore what the Spanish become when they are there: old ladies (ladies not women) with their mantillas and flowers meet and talk to everyone, the atmosphere, the noise, the beautiful dresses, the men in traditional costume, the Andalusian hats.

Because my husband is so mad about bullfighting every August we rent a loge for the full ten days of *feria*, which we share with twelve other couples. It is quite a spectacle. Those twelve women wear a new dress every day and they expect to be treated with luxury. They pamper themselves before and during this time with trips to the beautician and hairdresser; they wear designer clothes and wonderful jewellery and each day they are photographed for posterity. Their men wait upon them, serving them the food; it's curious. It is all very luxurious and very expensive; one seat costs three hundred euros a day. We have been sharing this loge with these people for many years now and still they do not consider themselves our friends. We spend ten days together, all day and all evening; we eat and drink together. The nearest we have ever had to an invitation home was last year when we all went back to someone's swimming pool and we took the left-over food with us, wrapped up in cartons and packed with ice. But we still did not go into their house.'

I asked her how she had come to live on the outskirts of Málaga.

'I developed breast cancer and I came to one of my father's clinics in Málaga for treatment: chemotherapy, radiation. Of course by then my father was dead,' she added. 'My husband said Almeria was too far away and that I should rent a place here while I was having treatment and he would run the business in Almeria. I rented a small house with one bathroom and no swimming pool but after eleven months the landlady threw me out. Three times this happened to me. I saw that nobody cared. Even in the clinic where I went every two days I was surprised how aggressive everybody was with me.

Anyway when they realised it was cancer the doctors decided to operate immediately and remove my breast. I insisted that they put in a prosthesis straight away. The surgeon warned against it but I was adamant; I said it would do me more psychological damage if it wasn't done. However they were right and after two years my body began to reject the prosthesis. I was very ill and had to have a ten hour operation to put it right. Then I said, OK that's it, finished. To fight cancer you have to have a strong mental attitude. I thought well up to now I have had a beautiful life so I am not going to let it make me depressed.

Then I decided to give up my rented accommodation and buy this house. We both agreed that we would wind down the company in Almeria and retire. It's in the process of being sold now.

This house is the first house I have lived in that I did not design. It was not very interesting but I have changed it all. Now we live here and commute to Almeria when we need to.'

I asked her if she was friends with any of the Spanish aristocracy. She shook her head.

'We don't have any contact with Spanish aristocracy; I think the Spanish aristocracy suffers from a complex. It's probably something to do with the time when Franco was in power. I do have one friend who is a doctor and she has more sympathy with us than other Spanish aristocrats.

I am very proud of my name and I try to uphold it whenever and wherever I can. Our family is thirteenth in the ranking of international aristocracy. We are on the same level as our cousins, the Grimaldis in Monaco. For example when the Prince of Monaco dies I will be expected to go to his funeral to represent our family. When his successor is nominated I will have to go and sign my name along with the other families to confirm his appointment. It is an obligation and if you want to continue to represent your family name you have to do it. My son and I are the only ones now with that name.

For me to be an aristocrat is to have a job. I remember my father said to me: "Be careful. You must be proud of your name and your roof." Do you know what an aristocrat is? It's someone who receives something, a domain, a field, a house, a castle and he must maintain it all his life; even though he has no money he must find a way of maintaining it. My father said: "Be careful Eve, remember that you must first spend your money to keep your roof intact."

My son lives in New Caledonia. He doesn't like his title and never uses it. Sometime soon I have to go to France to sell our domain and he has to sign as well; it's going to be a problem because I know he never likes to sign his full name. It's hard for him. Luckily it doesn't matter to me that he feels that way. If I was like others in our family I would cut him off but I am not like that. I love my son and my three grandchildren although I do not see them very often.'

Migrants and immigrants

Spain is no newcomer to migration; its history has seen both internal waves of migration, such as in the fifties and sixties when half a million people moved from the rural south to Catalunia and Barcelona in particular, and external migration. At the end of the nineteenth century almost four hundred thousand people emigrated to South and Central America. By 1901 people were leaving at the rate of 100,000 a year, many of them from the impoverished Galicia. From 1960 until the mid seventies almost three million people left to work in northern Europe.

At the same time the sixties saw the arrival of large numbers of Moroccans and Latin Americans, almost all were single men looking for work. By the mid eighties immigrant families started arriving. According to a census of foreign residents in 2000 Spain was home to almost 900,000 legal immigrants, a third of whom were from the European Union. An equal number of illegal immigrants were also thought to live there. By 2003 the National Institute of Statistics reported that the number of registered foreigners living in Spain had risen to 2,664,168 making up 6.2% of the population. The largest group of immigrants was from Ecuador, then Moroccans, Colombians and Britons. Although the British ex-pats numbered 161,000 the unofficial estimate was closer to 500,000. By 2006 immigrants counted for 8.75% of the population. They were mostly comprised by young adults aged between 25 and 44 years old. Only the British had a higher average age of 52 years.

The immigrants worked mainly in the areas of agriculture, construction, housework activities and the restaurant/food industry. On average they received poorer wages and worked in worse conditions than the Spanish. Very often they had no security of employment, were given only temporary contracts and were not enrolled in the Social Security system. It was estimated that about one third of all foreigners experienced a lower job satisfaction due to being over qualified for the work they were required to do.

In 2007 8.75% of the population were foreigners compared to 1.37% ten years previously. This change has had a number of consequences for Spanish society in terms of demography, economics and social implications. The supply of cheap, flexible labour is thought to have been a major contributor to Spain's economic growth during the last ten years.

Conclusion

After listening to many of the women interviewed it is obvious that during the period of Franco's dictatorship women's lives were controlled not only by their fathers and husbands but also the State and the Church. If you were lucky enough to have a good husband, like Araceli or Dolores, then you led a restricted but protected life, cherished and cared for by a loving man. However if, like Lola, you had a jealous, devious man as a husband your life could be a misery because there was no-one to turn to for help. With the death of Franco and the rise of democracy things began to change not least because enshrined in the new Spanish Constitution was the concept of equality for all regardless of sex, race or religion. The Spanish like to cling to their traditions but even the most traditional among them have now had to come to terms with the fact that in modern Spain women have equal rights with men.

Conclusion suggests finality, an ending to a process, but in fact this is a process which is forever changing; a metamorphosis that has yet to end. All we can say is that women in twenty-first century Spain are grabbing at life with both hands; they want to enjoy their lives to the full, be it as mothers, wives, career women, carers or a combination of them all. The restrictions that have held them back for years have been removed and now it is up to them to use their new freedom as they see best. The daughters of Spain can now develop and grow alongside their brothers.

APPENDIX 1
OTHER FAMOUS SPANISH WOMEN:

It is not surprising that the list of famous Spanish women is not very long, given the restrictions that they have lived under for so long. Most that have achieved fame have been singers, such as Victoria de los Ángleles and Montserrat Caballé, and actresses: Ana Belén and Penélope Cruz, all of whom are known internationally. There are also a few women who have earned their place in history: Augustina de Aragona, Queen Isabella, Maria Pita and Rosalia de Castro.

Isabella I of Castile 1451-1504
Isabella I was born in 1451 and reigned from 1474 to 1504. She was queen of Castile and Leon and when she married her husband Ferdinand II of Aragon, together they laid the foundation for the political unification of Spain. The Pope named them the "Catholic Monarchs" so she is often referred to as Isabella the Catholic.

1492 was an important year for Isabella because it saw the conquest of Granada, the last stronghold of the Moors and the end of the re-conquest campaign, "La Reconquista", the expulsion of the Jews from Spain and the start of her successful patronage of Christopher Columbus.

After rejecting Columbus's plan to sail west to the Indies three times, she at last agreed to give him the ships and money that he needed. When he returned the following year with gold and natives for her, Spain entered a Golden Age of exploration and colonisation. In 1494 the Catholic Monarchs divided the world outside of Europe between themselves and the King of Portugal. In 1503 she appointed a Secretary for

Indian Affairs, who later became incorporated into the Supreme Council of the Indies.

Not only did the Catholic Monarchs unite Spain physically but they tried to unite in spiritually as well, bringing the whole country under the Catholic Church. As part of this process the Inquisition became institutionalised.

Isabella and Ferdinand were an effective team and worked under equal terms. They had drawn up a pre-nuptial agreement that stated quite clearly that "Isabella and Fernando were equal"; there was no question of Ferdinand having more power than her. They unified Spain, reformed the church, concluded the Re-conquest, improved the armed forces and created a legal framework for the State. All that and Columbus's discoveries in the New World turned Spain into a world power.

Saint Teresa of Avila 1515-1582 Roman catholic mystic and monastic reformer

Maria Pita 1565-1643

In La Coruña there is a statue to Maria Pita, who became famous at the siege of La Coruña in 1589, when she extorted the citizens to defend themselves against the English Armada under Sir Francis Drake, with cries of: "Those with honour, follow me." She helped to tend the wounded and bury the dead. Married and widowed four times, she was awarded a pension by the King Felipe II and granted a licence to export mules from Spain to Portugal.

Maria de Zayas y Sotomayor 1590-1660
Maria de Zayas y Sotomayor was born in Madrid to a wealthy family. She was a contemporary of Cervantes and wrote two volumes of short stories about and for women. The stories were written from a woman's perspective, depicting clearly the injustices and abuses that women in all levels of society suffered at that time.

Augustina de Aragona 1786-1857
Augustina de Aragóna was born in Tarragona in 1786 and has become a folk heroine for generations of Spanish because of her heroic actions defending the city of Zaragosa during the Spanish War of Independence. She later became an officer with the allied forces under the Duke of Wellington and ultimately rose to the rank of captain. In 1813 she fought as a front line battery commander at the Battle of Vitoria, where the French army was finally destroyed. She became known as the "Spanish Joan of Arc", was the subject of a painting by Goya, entitled "The Disasters of War" and appears in the poem "Childe Harold" by Lord Byron. However recent research suggests that she was neither particularly pious nor patriotic, simply a girl attracted by war. Her actions would have been outlawed by the Catholic Church as more becoming to a witch than a heroine had it not been for the fact that they were encouraging all Spaniards to fight against the French captors of the divinely crowned King of Spain.

Rosalia de Castro 1837-1885
Rosalia de Castro was a poet and writer who wrote in both Spanish and Gallego. She played an important role in the resurgence of the Galicia language. Besides writing poetry she was a staunch defender of women's rights and was deeply

concerned about the poor. Despite bearing seven children she had no grandchildren.

Dolores Ibárruri 1895-1989

Dolores Ibárruri, also known as La Pasionaria, the passion flower, became known for her defence of the Republic in the Spanish Civil War. She coined the slogan "¡No pasarán!"during the Battle of Madrid, "They shall not pass!" Her speeches against fascism attracted large audiences and gained many supporters for the Republican cause, especially women. In 1942 she escaped from Spain and went into exile in the USSR. When Franco died she returned to Spain and was elected as a deputy to the Cortes in 1977.

Alicia de Larrocha 1923

Alicia de Larrocha y de Calle was born in Barcelona in 1923 and is widely considered to be the best pianist in Spain. She made her debut in the concert hall at the age of thirteen and from1939 played in concerts all over Europe. However it was in 1954 when she went to the United States that she achieved truly international fame.

Victoria de los Ángeles 1923-2005

Victoria de los Ángeles was born in Barcelona in 1923, the daughter of a university porter, and died in 2005. She began her career as a soprano at the age of eighteen. In 1945 she made her debut as the countess in the Marriage of Figaro and from then on her career flourished. She won international prizes and performed in London, Paris and Milan. In 1950 she went to United States for the first time. Despite her fame she never forgot her humble beginnings and never acted the part of the temperamental diva. She was married and had two children, one of whom had Down's Syndrome; in 1970 she and her husband separated. In 1996 she gave her last recital at the age of seventy-two.

Margarita Salas 1938
Margarita Salas was born in Asturias and at the age of sixteen moved to Madrid to study chemistry. Her career as a molecular biologist has been long and successful. She has won many research prizes for her work, such as UNESCO's Carlos J. Finley prize in 1992, the Jaime I Research Prize and in 1999 she won the UNESCO L'Oreal prize for the best European scientist. Since 1995 she has been Head of the Instituto de España.

She is quoted as saying that she believes that women will achieve a greater degree of participation in society but not through government quotas, which she is strongly against, but through their own efforts. As she says: "It's up to us to conquer the space that we deserve."

Arantxa Sánchez-Vicario 1971 tennis player
Ten Grand Slam titles winner

Conchita Martínez 1972 tennis player
1994 Wimbledon Women's Singles Champion

Cristina Sánchez 1972 bullfighter

Virginia Ruano 1973 tennis player
Eight Grand Slam Doubles titles

Tamara Rojo 1974 prima ballerina with London's Royal Ballet

Penélope Cruz 1974

Penélope Cruz is one of the best known Spanish actresses in the world, having made films in England, Italy, France and United States as well as in her native Spain. She was born into a working-class family in Madrid in 1974. When she saw the film "¡Atame!" directed by Pedro Almodóvar she decided she wanted to become an actress and work with him. Her dream came true and in 1997 she worked with Almodóvar for the first time in the film "Carne Trémula"; since then she has made many films with him, including starring in his film "Volver" for which she was nominated for an Oscar in 2006.

She speaks four languages: Spanish, French, Italian and English and now at the age of thirty-four has a long list of films and awards to her credit. She and her sister have also created a collection of clothes for one of the big Spanish clothing chains.

APPENDIX 2
SPANISH GOVERNMENTS 1931-2008

Spanish Second Republic 1931-1936
Democratic Government of the Popular Front 1936
Spanish Civil War 1936-1939
Dictatorship under Francisco Franco y Bahamonde 1939-1975
Parliamentary Monarchy King Juan Carlos 1975
Democratic Government 1977-1982
Spanish Constitution 1978
Democratic Government 1982-1996 Presidente Felipe González Márquez (PSOE)
Democratic Government 1996-2004 President José María Aznar López (PP)
Democratic Government 2004-2011 President José Luis Rodríguez (PSOE)
Democratic Government 2011- present President Mariano Rajoy Brey (PP)

APPENDIX 3
FURTHER READING

Laurie Lee "A Rose for Winter" 1955
Ronald Fraser "Blood of Spain" 1979
Giles Tremlett "Ghosts of Spain" 2006
Max Gallo "Spain Under Franco" 1969
Frances Lannon "Women & Images of Women in the Spanish Civil War"
Ivan Muzychka "Exploring Women's social service in Franco's Spain"
Conor McLoughlin "Free Women of Spain"
NATO/IMS Committee on Women in the NATO forces: Spain
Agnes Pardell "Women and Politics in Spain" 1997
"The Changing Attitudes in Spain"
"Anarchism in the Spanish Revolution"
Paul Hamilton "Spain's Divorce Rate soars" The Guardian 17th Nov 2007
John Hooper "The New Spaniards" 1995
Mireia Ferrer Alvarez "Historical Studies of the Practice and Profession of Women Artists"
Agnés Pardell "Women and Politics in Spain" 1997
Iñigo Isusi "Employment and Working Conditions of Migrant Workers – Spain" 2007
Shirley Mangini "Resistencia a la Memoria y Memorias de Resistencia" 1996
Dra. Mercedes Arríaga "Escritoras y Pensadoras Europeas" 2005